THE EMPEROR AND THE RING

Susan,
   Congrats on winning the giveaway. Book 3 in the trilogy was released in Dec, so if you like this book, the sequel is waiting on you.

JEFF GAURA

Trilogy Christian Publishers
A Wholly Owned Subsidiary of Trinity Broadcasting Network
2442 Michelle Drive
Tustin, CA 92780

Cover design by: Cornerstone Creative Solutions

Inside graphics and maps by: McKenna Kirkpatrick

For information, address Trilogy Christian Publishing
Rights Department, 2442 Michelle Drive, Tustin, Ca 92780.
Trilogy Christian Publishing/ TBN and colophon are trademarks of Trinity Broadcasting Network.

For information about special discounts for bulk purchases, please contact Trilogy Christian Publishing.

Manufactured in the United States of America

Trilogy Disclaimer: The views and content expressed in this book are those of the author and may not necessarily reflect the views and doctrine of Trilogy Christian Publishing or the Trinity Broadcasting Network.

10 9 8 7 6 5 4 3 2 1

Library of Congress Cataloging-in-Publication Data is available.

ISBN 978-1-63769-136-6 (Print Book)
ISBN 978-1-63769-137-3 (ebook)

to Lynn and Maggie

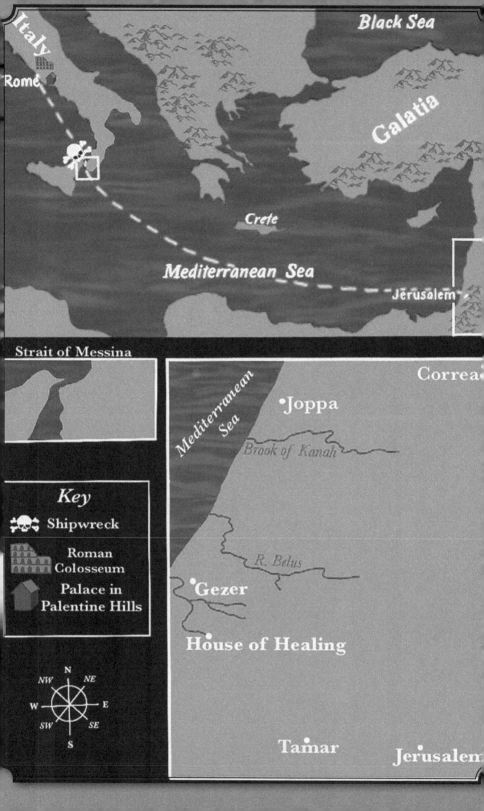

FOREWORD

An overwhelmingly dishonest theme coming from our history and religious teachers these days is that things are comparatively bad now and are only getting worse. Social unrest movements start with the mass distribution of the "things are bad" message using images on social and traditional media. Then, without knowing what it holds, they report to us with a matter-of-fact approach that the future is on a collision course to be worse than today. In essence, they convince us to sin, that we need to sin to make things right. We burn other people's property and throw things at them. We attack them with words and weapons, thinking it will help.

The younger the listener, the more likely they comply and contribute to the circle of dishonesty. It is sick, and there is nothing new about it.

As a part of writing this trilogy, I felt compelled to academically explore a day in the life of someone living in first-century Palestine. Before I finished the work of only two different authors, I realized that there is no doubt that modern Christianity and the people who claim it as their faith have it easy! Where do I start to compare the present to the first century? To begin, 25 percent of us are not slaves. Neither Jews nor Christians today are beheaded in public with 50,000 people watching down and laughing. I know of no places on earth where mass crucifixions occur, organized by highly trained engineers to address both the time requirements to kill several hundred people a day on limited soil and the requirements of the disposal of the bodies to minimize flies and pestilence. We have relatively no clue what it means to be repressed.

Ancient Israel in the time of the Roman Empire had all those things. To say that the Jews and Christians from Ancient Israel were oppressed is like calling Mount Everest "another big hill." Freedom under Roman rule was an all-or-nothing proposal. You either had all available freedom, or you had nearly none. Today, there are many shades of freedom, and the global middle class includes more than a billion individuals (and growing) who are Christ-followers. Our life spans are longer, our access to health care is advanced, our housing is safe, our transportation cheap, and we have universal education. Global poverty is at an all-time low since this has been a measurable event.

Each time I hear a preacher talking about how things are going in the wrong direction and have been for quite some time, I wish I could pick him up and dump him in ancient Israel for a month and then put him back in the pulpit, filming the entire event. Even the most eloquent of speakers would flop on their face when asked to compare the first century to the twenty-first century from a Christian perspective. We are in the golden age of freedom as Christ-followers. We are in the golden age of freedom as humans; do not let the uneducated fools of social unrest dupe you that we need to somehow repent from our past and change. The evidence is bulletproof. We have changed, and we are better. History proves this from all perspectives greater than a century or two at a time.

Yet, one point of greatest interest is consistent between those two times. Jesus works on one person at a time and one relationship at a time; relationships of eternal significance cannot be mass-produced. All of us get to know the One Person of God through something one of His current followers shared with us. It is always unique. It is always circumstantial. It changes eternity when it happens. In that sense, the first century is just like today.

My first date with Jesus happened when I was wearing a guitar on a stage at a US church. The pastor had asked for people to apply to become the new lead guitarist at a church I had attended exactly one time. They gave me the job, failing to ask me if I even believed in what they teach. I had just come back from a multi-year stint in the Peace Corps, and I was looking for a place to fit in. In my mind, I was being culturally sensitive. I knew that in rural South Carolina culture, a normal life included going to church on Sunday. After a couple of weeks of "performing" at the worship service, I had a personal experience with a Living God that I did not previously know. I cried on stage moments before I was to "perform" for several hundred people. Another member of what I called the "band," but what they called the "worship team," told me that the Holy Spirit was upon me.

In the way that God wants us all to have faith like a child, I complied, asking a question openly and with ignorance. "Who is the Holy Spirit?" I asked.

Dennis, the keyboard player, saw what was going on, and moments before we began a worship set of Maranatha music, I gave my life to Christ. Dennis thought the event was hysterical, and his laughter helped me stop crying long enough to play an opening riff for the first song. That day, I cannot tell you if my Fender Stratocaster was in tune or even if it was turned on. I just played, closed my eyes, and said, "Wow," as I heard the singer's words and connected with them for the first time in my life. I had been playing these types of songs for a month, and I was more concerned with the patterns I would play as we transitioned from D to A minor than the Creator of the universe for whom I was playing.

I still remember the colors of that moment. I remember the slope of that church's floor that I had to walk down and walk up as I transitioned from church member to lead guitarist and back. Certainly, that pastor got a grade of "F" for not screening me before giving me permission to lead his people in worship. Yet, is it not true that God can use all things for His glory, including the mistakes in church and the mistakes by the church? I claim to be the evidence that this is true. My characters in all three books in the Seeker's Trilogy reflect that heart of God.

This book is about a couple of adolescents who encounter life's tragedies and are forced to address the world on the world's terms, using their passion for adventure and the power of prayer. They navigate repression, but they also experience it and are damaged by it. They know they are damaged, too.

My creative mind saw a place in the history of the world to allow some unique events to be possible. I found real places on the map and included them. I found places on the map where there was nothing, and I made something up and put it there. I built upon what I had already done in the first book, as well. It was an easy story to develop, and I imagine the characters in this book from a third-person view, for which I am invisible. When the primary characters of this book are alone, I imagine myself talking to them and guiding their choices as best as I can. That is what Christ does. That is what my parents did while they were alive.

My closest circle of friends is in the latter years of their lives, and I often talk to them about what goes on in the head of Jeff, the writer. I think about the legacies that they will be leaving when their bodies fail, and they depart this world to enter eternity. Part of their tales have inspired me to write, for I perceive that I will outlive all of them; at least, that is what the actuaries tell us. My prayer is that my passion for writing does not waiver as I lose them from my circle. They are irreplaceable to me.

I hope you like this representation of our faith's history. This remains a fictional tale. Book three is complete, and I aim to release it under the same publisher sometime in 2021.

Jesus is right here, right now. I love the colors that He uses when He operates. They look good on me.

PROLOGUE

Recorded History and context

It is now AD 81. Less than fifty years have passed since Yeshua has died. Since the destruction of the Temple almost fourteen years earlier, the members of The Way have now called themselves "Yeshuaians," and their numbers are growing all around the world. However, Roman authority continued to grow and expand, and much of the wealth stored in the Second Temple has been lost or taken back to Rome for use in Roman public work projects under Vespasian's son, Titus.

Israel was now a separate unit of administration in the eyes of Rome called *Provincia Judaea*. Hebrews spoke the name "Israel" amongst themselves, but in the common tongue of Greek, the land in which they lived was now called Judah by all. It was a crime to call it by its older name.

Taxes were collected and sent to Rome, but under Titus, Judah's tax burden was reduced. Titus replaced his father Vespasian in AD 79, almost twelve years after sacking Jerusalem and destroying the Second Temple of King Solomon. Although many feared that Titus would be ruthless, he was found to be a great leader and open to new ideas. His reign was short-lived, and he died of what were believed to be natural causes. He was succeeded by his younger brother, Domitian.

Synopsis of Book 1

Yeshua came and left, and the Roman Empire remained in control of Judah. Emperors changed many times after the death of Yeshua, but the Roman power and authority did not. Some people followed the message shared by the Messiah, but most dismissed the stories of His time on earth, as not all the promises of the prophets had been fulfilled by His deeds while He was living.

A teenage girl from a Hebrew village in the northern territories of Israel succumbs to the sin of fornication and decides, on the night of her old sister's wedding, to atone for her sins. She takes minimal supplies and sets out on foot in the middle of the night to reach Jerusalem and make a sacrifice at the Second Temple of King Solomon. According to the Torah, this act of penance will rid her of the guilt and shame caused by her fornication, and she will be able to start life anew and perhaps one day get married to a nice Hebrew man like her sister did.

After viewing unspeakable acts on her six-day journey to the Holy City, she arrives outside the walls of the famed city, only to find the city surrounded and closed off by Roman legions, set on destroying the city as a penalty for defiance against the emperor's claims of authority. The Roman military barred the city gates for three months, allowing no one in or out, as they starved the city into submission. Yael cannot atone for her past without trying to find a way inside, and she sets out in the middle of the night to find a back door entrance. She stumbles upon one of the many hidden tunnels from the days of King David that lead into the city and travels under the city, only to find herself face to face with Mishi, a young rabbi who was building a bunker under the temple to keep the Romans from finding him. She insists that she be allowed to participate in the ritual of atonement to free her of guilt and give her the ability to start life anew, but there are no animals left to sacrifice. The young rabbi cannot help her with her grief but listens to her confession, and the two of them connect. He also confesses that it was sinful for him to hide food and supplies when the people who worked at the Temple school were starving to death. She escapes back out of the city at night, hoping to buy an animal and secretly bring it back into the city using the tunnels and rid herself of the guilt her sin brought upon her.

After she leaves the city through the hidden tunnel she found, she is raped by a Roman guard early one morning. Unknowingly, she becomes pregnant. The same day she is raped, the Romans begin their siege on Jerusalem, and she watches the city and the Temple destroyed.

Back inside the city, Mishi is taken prisoner when the Romans enter the Temple grounds, and he becomes a slave of Rufus. Rufus is the son of the centurion Cornelius from Caesarea and the second in command of the siege. He is a legate, overseeing an entire legion of five thousand Roman soldiers, and he is present during the destruction of the Temple. Rufus engages Mishi and finds the young Jew to be both intellectual and highly social, and Rufus asks him to inquire about what truths may exist in the stories he had heard that there was a new King on Earth named Yeshua.

The two of them simultaneously explore the idea together and find evidence that the claims are true.

Meanwhile, an old woman comforts Yael, and she finds her way to the underground synagogue of the followers of The Way, and she reconnects with Mishi. The two of them are then commissioned by a wounded traveling doctor who had firsthand experience of Yeshua and his follower Paul. The doctor commissions the two of them to transcribe his message, and they make multiple copies to send to the small and floundering churches within the empire. These writings become the book of Luke and the Acts of the Apostles.

As Mishi and Yael work together in the days after the fall of Jerusalem, Mishi falls in love with Yael, even though she is pregnant with another man's child. Although it is unthinkable for a rabbi to marry a woman who was pregnant, he recounts the story of how Yeshua's birth came to pass, and he enters into *erusin*, or engagement, with Yael in a most public manner. Rufus is offered a chance to retire from the Roman military and stay behind, and he takes this opportunity. Once he leaves the Roman military, he has no need for wealth or fame and voluntarily takes a job as Mishi's and Yael's guide and protector. He helps distribute copies of the transcriptions that Yael and Mishi completed, and he escorts them all back to Yael's hometown. Her *erusin* with Mishi is now complete, and the two of them plan to marry. While there, Mishi tells the village the story of Yeshua, and many are saved. Yael tells her sister that she is pregnant, and her sister tells her that she also is.

Book two, *The Emperor and The Ring*, continues more than thirteen years later when Titus is the emperor, and it is his second year of Roman leadership.

THE COMPLICATIONS OF BEING A CELEBRITY RABBI'S SON

"Little One, come in to help with dinner!" yelled Yael from the door to their home. Their home and the synagogue next door were small, but both were quaint and clean. The day was overcast, and it never did warm up enough for her to go outside without her thick cloak and a scarf. Winter should be leaving this part of ancient Judah, but it hadn't left yet. Living near the edge of a desert meant sparse vegetation and limited water, but it also made the cold season short-lived. Either way, she needed her son's help to finish the preparations. Company would be arriving soon, and she couldn't do everything.

As Caleb approached her, Yael smiled and reached out her free arm to wrap it around her son as he entered the doorway, while her other hand lifted a small basket of vegetables that she intended to cook that evening. He was more than a full head taller than her, but that did not deter her from trying to wrap her cloak around him.

"Your father has been sitting at the feet of some of the leaders from Pergamon all day, and he sent a message that we will have three more guests with us for dinner and bed. They will be staying, and I need you to make sure that our extra room is swept clean and that the mats are aired out, along with the blankets and pillows. Put an extra one in there, too. With all these people coming and going in our home these days, I do not know what I would do without you. I really need to get those things down to the river to clean one of these days," she said, turning around and leaving him before she finished the last sentence. He hated how she would walk away from him while still talking to him.

Caleb bowed his head respectfully and took off his sandals, leaving them outside the door to the room, as all Hebrew boys are taught to do. He felt the cool air that came with walls made of dried straw and mud in their desert home. Although this task was purposeful, his mother also often gave him impromptu chores meant to make him stay near the house and synagogue. But he did not want to be there as much as she wanted him to be there. He liked to explore the deserts and the forest, track and hunt game, fish, shoot his bow, and get lost discovering Yahweh's creation. Yet he knew his mother made sacrifices for everyone, and this was the least that he could do for her.

Deep down, Caleb thought his mother gave him these chores because of her disdain for his desire to hunt. She never let him finish the stories of him tracking prey. His mother saw no difference between the beheading of a Jew and the cleaning of wild game, but Caleb saw the differences. Fortunately, his uncle did too. Uncle Rufus tried to console him when he went to him after feeling rejected by his mother. Rufus told the young man that his mother was very much like other mothers, trying to protect their children from the atrocities of the world. Caleb had only known one mother, so he just had to agree with him.

Caleb was now nearly a man, and he most certainly looked like a man. Despite his young age of thirteen years, Caleb already was taller than most men, and he was more muscular than even a highly trained Roman soldier. He was still a school-aged boy, but he was both taller and thicker than either of his parents. Most boys get tall first, then thicker later. Caleb grew both up and out concurrently. Rufus taught Caleb the exercise routine he used when he served as a legate in the Roman military some thirty years ago, and Caleb practiced it on most days. And it was Rufus who taught Caleb to hunt. Hunting with Rufus was what Caleb loved the most.

What really caught the attention of many of the people who came to the synagogue to learn from his parents wasn't his size but his grooming habits. Caleb kept his hair short like the Egyptians did, but he also sported a thick and shortly trimmed beard and mustache. He would visit an Egyptian barber when he was away from their village to get his hair cut and hear stories of life in ancient and modern Egypt. The barber gave him compliments on his beard and taught him how to trim it.

His father would go with him to the Egyptian barber, often wearing his rabbi apparel for no other reason than to start a conversation about why his son was getting a haircut. That always lead to a conversation about the Messiah, and his dad never had to push anyone into listening to him, even though everyone knew him as the former headmaster of the Temple Mount school. For them, Mishi's approach to Caleb represented about as big a shift as did the inclusion of the message of Yeshua in the synagogues around Judah. After all, children of rabbis were expected to look the part of a rabbi and the old sect of Pharisees before them. Caleb's father never pressed those sorts of expectations on him. Mishi taught him that the Messiah came for all, including those with different hairstyles, and we are saved by grace and through grace. That meant he could have any hair type he wanted, which included short hair and a beard.

Mishi, on the other hand, kept the appearance as any other Hebrew rabbi would, especially considering his role as mentor for many of the leaders for the newer Yeshuaian synagogues in Judah. He grew a long beard and covered his head at all times he wasn't in bed or bathing. Mishi's story of learning about Yeshua was common knowledge, and everyone who came to their synagogue was told that he and his wife would tell them their story at dinner. That meant Caleb would have to listen to the fall of the Temple and the Roman sack of Jerusalem again that night.

Nearly all who were inside Jerusalem when the Temple was destroyed either were enslaved or fled for their lives. Mishi and his *erusin* stayed around and helped to rebuild their faith. They established a school not just for students but for future Yeshuaian leaders to offer some formal education in the message of Yeshua revealed to all the remaining synagogues who would listen. Soon thereafter, Rufus, the retired legate of one of the legions that lead the sacking of Jerusalem, joined The Way and ceremonially became Caleb's uncle through a Hebrew tradition. Many others in the Roman army became followers of The Way in the weeks following the destruction of the Temple, and some of them had since gone back to Rome and started Yeshuaian synagogues in the capital city. Yeshuaian synagogues were now found nearly everywhere in the Roman Empire, even though the penalty for publicly denying worship to the emperor was death.

Caleb did like hearing tales of those who came from faraway places, but for the most part, those tales were brief, as men came to Tamar to listen to his father and mother and not talk to them. For every new story, he had to listen to ten old ones. Caleb yearned not just to visit these faraway places but to explore them. He wanted to walk their mountains, fish their rivers and lakes and track new and interesting game.

Even though his mother did not understand him, his father did.

"Abba, you want me to know the Creator," Caleb would say.

"Yes, I do. In what ways do you get to sense Him and experience Him?" Mishi would ask.

"I love creation, even though it is fallen from its original grandeur. I feel like I can see the Creator in creation better than I can in school. I want to visit and explore those places that you have talked about. I want to see the pyramids and the great volcanos. I want to see these churches and islands around the empire. I want to visit Gaul and Britannia, too. That would be my dream," Caleb would add.

The two of them compromised by insisting that he do both. His father would sometimes walk with him, and he would pray that Caleb finds his ministry in the places that *Yahweh* had called him.

"Abba, I am pretty sure that God has called me to serve Him outside the walls of a synagogue," Caleb would say, leading both of them to laugh. They both knew that one day, his prayer would be answered. That is how a living Messiah works.

Most onlookers concluded that Caleb was a strong and gifted young man. What they did not know was his desire to have a great adventure. People sometimes thought him to be more Roman soldier than Jew. The soldiers who had been dispatched to Palestine to observe the "rebel province" of Judah did not want to be there. Yet, all the soldiers that regularly patrolled their village knew of and respected his uncle, and his uncle had trained Caleb in many of their ways.

No Roman soldier, even his uncle Rufus, could catch him in a footrace of any distance, as the weight of their armor and his familiarity with the surroundings around Tamar made it impossible for him to be caught without a group effort. He was more than adept with a bow and gladius, so very few Roman soldiers mandated that Caleb follow the Roman rules to the letter. As such, he was allowed to travel openly displaying weapons, camp anywhere, and not pay a tax when he caught fresh game.

Caleb would go hunting at every chance. His hunting passion started when Uncle Rufus asked him to go with him one morning, and their routine of hunting a few times each week never stopped. Caleb looked forward to hunting treks with his uncle, even as a young boy. Even though neither of them could talk while they waited for game to arrive, the trip to the hunting area and the return were great story-telling opportunities. Caleb could listen to Uncle Rufus all day as he described the sieges he participated in while he was in the Roman military. Caleb loved to hear about Britannia and Gaul the most, as the people and the places seemed so different than life in occupied Judah. The tales of everyday rain on the island of Britannia were perhaps the most unbelievable of all to a boy coming from a desert.

Even on the days when there was not game to hunt, Uncle Rufus would help him practice his archery skills, as well as to wield a gladius. Rufus had joined The Way and become a disciple of Yeshua, but he could not discard the value of his twenty-plus years of military. He took ownership of safeguarding travel when Caleb's parents would leave Tamar to speak and instruct at distant synagogues in the ways of Yeshua. Rufus was one of many Hebrew leaders who thought much of Paul's troubles and imprisonment could have been prevented with better personal protection, and he kept his soldiering skills sharp to protect Mishi and Yael from any violent act. It certainly did not hurt being a retired leader of 5,000 Roman soldiers and the former best friend of the current emperor. Intimidation kept the sword from use better than any other Roman military art in Rufus's arsenal of weapons.

For Rufus, the best part of mentoring Caleb wasn't that he found his calling of spreading the kingdom of God using the skills from his military service. The best part of his new life was that Caleb wanted to learn all about his old life.

"My boy, it is sometimes said that when the student is ready, the teacher appears. You have inverted this for us. I believe the teacher was ready first, but the teacher did not know it!" Rufus would say, laughing and hugging Caleb as if he were his own son.

The hunting gave Caleb something else to think about other than the topics the rabbis taught him in school. Seldom did the rabbis teach them with authority that came from experience. Most of them were rabbis in training, or at least that was the title his mother called them. He knew that his parents were using their local school to train the next generation of teachers, and everyone wanted to learn about the Messiah from the people who transcribed His words. There always seemed to be more rabbis in Tamar than any other place that he ever visited.

Caleb had no interest in becoming the public orator that his father and mother were. Yet, he loved listening to them tell stories to large crowds, and he picked up many of their tricks to engage people. His parents were experts at winning an argument. His father and mother both knew how to use small words to cause big changes in people's hearts. He loved watching them do that. He just did not know how to do it himself.

"Your mom and dad have a great way with words, young man," Uncle Rufus would tell him. "The world needs to hear their stories, and I am here to help them tell those stories and not get killed for trying. It's my job to keep them protected and safe, and the words I use and the weapons I carry are some of my tools." That was how Rufus would describe his allotments of weapons and the mercenaries he employed to help escort Caleb's parents as they traveled to other synagogues to share their message. "When your mother was writing down what Rabbi Luke told her, all three of us decided that spreading the message of Yeshua did not require the path of suffering that Paul used. Your parents did not need to get stoned, thrown in prison, and physically attacked when they proclaimed Yeshua to be the Messiah. My men and I escort them when they go places to make sure they get a chance to tell the Greatest Story." Caleb thought that he would love to be a part of Rufus's team of protectors one day.

His father's story-telling skills were mesmerizing. Perhaps that skill was what made him a celebrity in the new faith. He never took any credit for the content of his stories, always referencing whose words he was repeating, but Caleb watched many people begin to understand the sacred Torah and how Yeshua fulfilled God's promises, especially when the Temple collapsed. Uncle Rufus never spoke at these gatherings, but his dad often discussed Rufus's pathway to salvation while he was in the room as they traveled to distant lands. There were no more than ten legates in the world at any time, and every Roman and Hebrew in attendance over the age of thirty knew who Rufus was. It was a big deal to all of the doubting Jews that a Roman legate had joined their lot and followed The Way. Some distant synagogues would send their leaders to Tamar for training, and upon return to their homes and villages, their first story was often that Rufus was among them.

It was not common knowledge that Rufus's best friend in adolescence was Titus, who was now the Roman emperor. Caleb would often press him on the subject of that relationship, and Rufus indulged him with stories of his and Titus's antics during their years serving together. Caleb never heard Rufus telling those stories to his mother and father. He wondered if they already knew them or did not want to know them.

His father had not only made peace with the destruction that Rufus created in his life but loved the man for it. His father's story nearly always included a message of great hope to the people listening.

"Yeshua came to save us from the tyranny not of Roman law but of our own law and our sin. He came to save us from our sins and crimes against each other. You can follow Halakha law regarding your hair, your clothes, your incense, and your bathing habits, but I am going to follow the saving message of Yeshua. My brother over there is known to you as the one who destroyed King Solomon's Second Temple. Yet what he did fulfilled what the prophets told us was required to come to pass for others to believe. This man eats in my house, serves in our synagogues, and keeps us safe. The Messiah offers a pathway for all who come to know Him. The Messiah came not just for the Jews. He came for Roman soldiers too."

Mishi would then summarize his story with Rufus while the crowd listened in amazement. "Once the Temple fell, I was taken, and I became his slave. In the days that followed, we each had powerful encounters with the Living God. He then freed me from slavery on earth, and Yeshua freed us both from the slavery of sin. We both joined The

Way. We met with Rabbi Luke, whose hands were damaged. He asked my wife and me to transcribe his words regarding Yeshua and his message of hope and wonder. We wrote every word he said, and we read them back to him. With the help of my other students, we recorded several copies, and this man lead the distribution of them amongst the tribes and nations of the world. None of these things could have happened without this Roman. I tell you: this man before you today is no different from you or me. Yes, he has done bad deeds. However, with Yeshua, we need only believe in Him as our Savior, and things are made right for us."

His mother stepped back into the guest room, interrupting his daydream.

"Son, your father is here with his guests." Yael's words interrupted Caleb's wandering thoughts. "I need you to wash their hands and feet with water before we serve them dinner."

His mother's tone declared that this wasn't a negotiation. He knew that it would be dishonorable not to comply with her heartfelt request. After all, he was the son of both a traditional male rabbi and the first female rabbi at a Hebrew school in recorded history. Caleb grabbed a towel, a bowl, and a large pitcher of water and walked out of the house towards the end of their porch, where the men would soon be arriving.

His mother spoke from behind as he approached his father and his father's peers from the Island of Cyprus and the new church there. "Thank you, my son. You make your father and me proud."

"Of course," he said and bowed his head.

He wanted to do what God made him to do. What was wrong with that? But when would she ever listen to stories about hunting?

ON CORREAE'S SECRET

Katya and Matthew had made a wonderful life considering they lived in an occupied land. Their small Hebrew village of Correae had doubled in size since they had married, and it now supported nearly a hundred families. In the thirteen years since she had given birth, her daughter had grown into a mature adolescent young woman. The village footprint had expanded, as there was a need to grow more food to feed more mouths. In addition, their village synagogue could now afford to hire more than one rabbi to teach the children. Despite this growth, the center of the village where the children played, festivals were celebrated, and the elders decided on communal affairs had not changed in size. It seemed like kids were outside screaming and chasing each other during all waking hours.

With the village growth, there were sometimes as many as four rabbis concurrently teaching the Hebrew children and the children of their slaves. Katya and Matthew shared the same school experience together, and all of Correae's residents received more education than nearly all Roman citizens and most Jews. After all, this hamlet was extremely wealthy, as they mined a secret vein of gold outside the village on the river. It required an educated and organized workforce to mine, smelt, mold, and distribute the precious metal without drawing the attention of the Roman Empire.

All this growth was not organic, nor was it caused by events of a predictable nature. When the Second Temple was destroyed by Roman armies, the economy it supported collapsed along with it. There were no longer street merchants selling to pilgrims coming to the Temple to atone for their sins. The quaint inns and food services within walking distance of the Temple grounds disappeared in a flash. Those who worked in that industry had to leave to find work, and some of them ended their journey in Correae, a six-day walk from the City of David. These migrant workers traveled north to the end of the road to restart their lives. However, since it was near the northernmost edge of Judah, only a small handful of escaping Jerusalem Jews ever reached this village. Correae was isolated because there was only one path into the village that supported carts, wagons, and caravans. Most who arrived did not even spend the night, as there was no inn for transients. But a few of them arrived with essential provisions, and they went to work. They engaged the community leaders in a humble enough manner so as to receive a plot of land on loan so they could camp, farm, and eventually build a home. Most slept under the stars and lived on whatever reserves they brought with them.

The Romans used starvation to destroy the spirit of the residents of Jerusalem before breaking through the walls and tearing down the Temple. As such, most of those still alive within the city walls lacked the physical strength to make the journey from Jerusalem to Correae. Of those who were strong enough to make the journey, a small group were members of The Way, the newly founded Hebrew sect that Katya's sister and brother-in-law helped lead.

Although many migrants arrived and then immediately left, some stayed and worked for a few days for food and a few shekels at harvest time. The lack of permanent work discouraged most of them, seeing life in Correae as a dead-end. A select few made the journey after hearing stories of Correae from Katya's sister and brother-in-law as a place of great hope. These people arrived with a spark in their eyes, willing to work hard. They were grateful for a chance to start their lives again in a place where the idea of a risen Messiah was respected. Once they accumulated enough wealth to pay back the loan used to buy their land and build their home, they were well-received by the village leaders, and they quickly melded into the community. It was common for the community to hold a celebration when a family climbed out of their debt, and they would be celebrated with gifts and a huge community meal.

There was no way for the migrants to determine the source of all the hidden wealth upon arrival. Correae was geographically hidden by design, and there were no plans to build a second road into or out of the village. Their secret was not disclosed to any travelers, regardless of circumstance.

Those who camped, built homes and decided to settle into a long-term life in Correae needed to prove their loyalty before they learned of the presence of gold and how the village managed that wealth. It was Matthew's job to screen those who stayed, learn their personal stories, and share his findings with the elders. If the elders selected a traveler to become a citizen, it was Matthew's job to teach them what responsibilities came with that citizenship. He would also lead them on their first tour of the gold mining operation, ever studying their facial features and non-verbal responses to see how much they could be trusted. The elders trusted Matthew's judgment in this area. He was able to read people and their motives better than anyone who had ever taken the responsibilities of this job.

The mine needed only a small number of people to operate, as the value of gold had increased under Roman occupation. The seasonal laborers worked only in the fields. Only the most trusted and time-tested of Jerusalem migrants, those who had been properly screened by Matthew, worked in the gold mines. After all, it only takes one greedy man or woman to ruin this experience for all the residents of the village.

THE LOVE OF A HUSBAND

Matthew was reminded by the elders several times each season that the survival of the village was contingent on his successful screening of refugees and migrants. If Matthew missed even one detail in their habits or how they responded to stress, the entire village could be doomed by a simple slip of the tongue.

The truth was that Matthew did not consider his job to be the most important part of his life in Correae. He saved the title of "most important job" for his role as husband to Katya. He spent much of his time patrolling the village perimeter and was keenly aware that if there were an attack by Romans against their village, he would be one of the first ones engaged in battle with the enemy. And he would be one of the first to die. He was not a well-trained soldier, either.

He and Katya lived in a well-kept but small home next to her parents, very close to the commons. His father-in-law and he were required by Hebrew tradition to complete the construction of that home before he was allowed to marry Katya. As such, his efforts to make that structure into their home were his top importance. It was in his efforts to build that home that he showed Katya his feelings for her. Ever since that event, all of his labor he considered a gift to his bride. Their daughter grew up hearing her father tell her mother of his love for her before he left for work. Those were also special moments for Katya. Matthew only spoke one word for every ten that Katya spoke, her mother would say, but his words filled her soul, and she treasured them. Her favorite moments were when he left and when he came home, as that was when he most filled her soul.

"My Katya, I am off to work. While I am gone, I will think about you and remember you. Love is not a strong enough word for what I feel for you. While I am away, coming home will be the most important act I perform each day. I promise never to take you for granted, and I want to be next to you as much as I can once I return."

As he would stand in front of her before turning to walk away, she would open her soul in the attempt to reciprocate the warmth that he shared. Yet, his words were of a depth that she could never equal. As he departed her, she would say, "You are a good man, Matthew." He knew this, but her simple affirmation meant as much to him as his words to her. She knew from her conversations with her friends that not every woman had a husband that adored her. She was not about to lose that connection.

Katya was beautiful and strong by any standards. She had perfect olive skin and deep green eyes with a beautiful smile that endeared her to everyone she met. People found themselves amazed at how quickly they felt comfortable enough to share with her from their heart. She had light brown hair, just like her sister, and perfectly straight white teeth, a feature that was most uncommon in Judah. Being a native-born citizen of Correae also meant that she grew up eating a lavish variety of foods, as the village wealth implied that there was a lot of imported food to keep them healthy and strong, even during the dry season.

Her strength was of the kind common for women who had been born and raised in Correae. As her contribution to the village, she had spent many days lifting and carrying raw ore baskets from the edge of the river to the smelting furnaces. The only path from the mine to the smelting place was through the river, walking upstream. She developed a good sense of balance as she carried heavy baskets of rocks in the seasonal currents of the Jabbok river. As such, neither cold water nor heavy loads concerned her.

Yet, that toughness did not prepare her for the adversity that is a part of marriage and parenting. It was now time to have a conversation about sending off Eliza to her sister, Yael, and brother-in-law, Mishi, again. For the last three years, Eliza spent fifteen six-week intervals living with her relatives. During the day, she studied in their Hebrew school; after school and on their day off, she helped them with household chores. After these six weeks ended, she would come home for one to two weeks. Eliza learned many skills that Katya never did, like speaking common Greek and using the vernacular and the accent of a Roman. However, during all this travel and spending nights in cities along the way, Eliza had also acquired the love of travel and adventure. And the last time she came home, she did so before her escort was ready, and she traveled across the land of Judah alone. That disregard of safety angered everyone both in Tamar and Correae.

However, she made it home without any negative consequence, and she was alive with stories of the people she met and the events she experienced on the way home. Her family did not know until the next day that she traveled alone, as she arrived at the end of dinner, and she spent nearly all of dinner telling tales of her time away. No one asked here where the escort was. For that, her mother and father both felt guilty for not reprimanding her for an apathetic approach towards safety.

The next morning when Katya learned that her daughter traveled six days alone on foot, she was furious. However, in her rage, she saw how well-adjusted her daughter looked, and she changed her mind and did not really know what she felt about Eliza's decision. It brought back memories of her younger sister.

Katya decided that her daughter was old enough to hear their family's secret story. Since Eliza was beginning to rebel against the absolute nature of authority, she needed to know what those who had come before her did.

After the morning meal, Katya left the job of cleaning up to their slaves. She turned to Eliza and said, "Let's take a walk." The two of them left and began traveling up the hills behind the village, away from where everyone else was coming and going. Neither the agricultural fields nor the mining operations were in this direction, and it was rocky and seldom traveled. Once they had walked about five minutes, Katya sat her daughter down on a large boulder that had some snow on it and told her daughter a story.

"Little One, your aunt knows this path better than I ever will, as I never go much higher than this."

"I do not know if I have ever come this high with the lions living up here," Eliza said, showing a bit of concern.

"I promised you a story, so here it is. Your aunt walked up here and far beyond, and it required a strong dose of courage. She wanted me to go with her, but I was too scared to go. She used to tell me she wanted to go high enough to see the great river Jordan. I thought she was being stupid, but she was serious. One time, she talked the son of our rabbi teacher into taking the hike with her. Once they reached the top of the hill, she consented to relations with him. He left the village the next day, and she was devastated." Katya waited to see what her daughter's reaction would be, but she couldn't read her. She counted to five before she added, "So, young lady, that was the first time Yael went traveling without a village escort."

"But mom, I would never think about doing that."

Katya had recently had a conversation with her daughter as to how procreation works, and she considered telling her daughter all of this at that time, but she withheld it.

"Perhaps not, but sins like that tend to keep themselves secret. I did not know any of that story until she was pregnant with your cousin. But that event really upset your aunt. She told no one for over a year. Then, during the night your father and I got married, Yael asked our father for his gold coins so she could travel to the Temple in Jerusalem to offer a sacrifice as is commanded in the sacred scrolls. She sought to restore herself before the eyes of Yahweh before she could restore herself to our family. She embarked to Jerusalem alone, in the night, while the rest of the village celebrated our wedding."

Eliza was taken aback, and Katya gave her time to process the story before continuing. Eliza held her face in her hands while her mother continued. Her mother paused while she let her daughter cry tears of education.

"When your aunt was on the way to that city, she had to watch the beheading of innocent Jews by the Romans, and she was raped by a Roman soldier. However, it was during that time, she met your uncle Mishi, and I know she has told you that story, hasn't she?"

"She did tell me that story, yes!" Eliza said, relieved to have something positive to talk about.

"You know what makes your aunt so amazing is the part of the story that you do not know, but it is time for you to know. She became pregnant by that Roman soldier, yet your uncle Mishi still decided to marry her and take her as his wife. He could have had her stoned for her insidious act to become pregnant out of *erusin* or wedlock. Instead, you know what he did? He forgave her, showing all of us how deeply the Messiah forgave us for our sins. I tell you right now that your uncle's act..."

She paused to wipe a tear from her own eye.

"Your uncle's act to take my sister as his bride and treat her like royalty, just as your father treats me, is worthy of..."

With that, her mother stopped, turned towards her daughter, and embraced her in a hug.

"My sister and I have been blessed to marry such honorable men! Your father and I want the same thing for you!" she said, holding her daughter by the cheek. She continued.

"Your aunt and uncle reflected the faith that they taught us about, and it was their combined commitment to the revelation that the Messiah has come that convinced your father and I that they were telling the truth."

"Your aunt delivered the child that was created by the Roman Soldier, and that is your cousin Caleb."

"Mom! Caleb really isn't my cousin?" was all Eliza could say.

"Oh, he is your cousin as much as Yael and Mishi are your aunt and uncle. Caleb has been raised as the son of a rabbi. Your aunt and uncle have happily shown the world what it means to be a Yeshua follower, and the two of them have literally changed all of Judah. I tell you the truth, Little One."

"Little one" is a term of greatest endearment in Hebrew. Its use indicates family or closeness. Katya only used it when she was trying to make points that she wanted her daughter to attach to her heart and carry through life.

"Mom. I had no idea."

Katya put a hand on each side of her daughter's face and looked her in the eyes, with tears coming from her own. "When I hear that you are traveling alone, I think of all the bad and all the good that happened to your aunt as a result of going into the unknown. I do not want anything other than good for you. You know that, right? For your aunt, the good was greater than the bad. I do not want the bad to be bigger than the good for you."

Both of them were now crying.

"Mom, but Caleb..." Eliza started, but her mother stopped her.

"You must never treat Caleb any differently than you do today. Do you hear me? The two of you have grown up together, and your aunt and I visited each other many times every year so you two could play together and be raised together. He is your family as much as I am," she waited for her daughter to respond. Eliza nodded.

"He is a Hebrew and was chosen by God to carry on our traditions, no matter what his blood is. Do you understand me?" Katya spoke with a seldom-used authoritarian tone. She had always felt a sense of guilt that her little sister was raped, and she had been unable to help. A part of that anger and self-loathing was becoming visible now.

"I'm sorry, Mother," she said. Eliza put her head on her mother's chest and began to cry steadily. Despite all of the female traits that puberty had bestowed upon her, she remained a little girl during this reveal. Katya knew that Eliza's love of a great adventure was a mirror image of her aunt's passion. As a woman living in an isolated Hebrew village, she had not yet decided if this was a curse or a blessing.

As a woman who had not experienced much of the world, she was not yet willing to admit she was jealous of her daughter's courage to tackle the unknown, one step at a time.

Yael had been a few years older than Eliza when she had left for Jerusalem, and the animosity between Rome and Judah was different and more structured now. Many in the village considered Eliza one of the best negotiators in foreign marketplaces, and she had been known to accompany other families when it was time to negotiate a larger-scale trade. This was good for the village, but it encouraged Eliza to step beyond the boundaries normally set for Hebrew girls entering womanhood. Katya knew Eliza could handle herself in any non-violent situation, but she was concerned about how her daughter would behave if threats and swords were involved.

But it wasn't her toughness in the marketplace that was on her mind. Eliza was physically smaller and younger than her aunt. She would be an easy target for a drunk Roman soldier, and that unknown scared her mother.

"Mother, I want to honor our family. I won't do anything to endanger us," she said as her tears came to an end.

"I know you do not want to do that," is what Katya told her. But, when it comes to things like rape and pillage, she had no experience to fall back upon. She helped her daughter stand back up, and they returned to Correae.

It was time to seek out the counsel of her husband. The entire family needed to talk about the good and the bad of traveling alone during the Roman occupation. Katya knew her husband Matthew's opinion would be the deciding factor.

Eliza Sees Her First Rainbow

Eliza knew better than to raise her voice, but she was on a precipice of saying something she would regret. She spoke up, but not with anger. She used a tone of authority like she had heard her mother use yesterday. It was the same tone her aunt used when she was teaching a room full of young men who challenged her authority as a female teacher of the ancient scrolls. Even though she was the scribe on the original writing of the message of the Messiah, many still thought Yael to be in an "improper position within the community of teachers."

"I have made the trip between here and Tamar fifteen times!" Eliza exclaimed. "I know every step of the road, what to look out for, where to stay, where to eat, and how long it takes. Uncle Mishi and Aunt Yael have taught me how to talk to Romans outside of our village. I speak better Greek than either of you two. I can even use their accent, Father! I have done this so many times! I do not need an escort anymore."

Eliza was making the case to travel back to school by herself. She wanted to ride her horse to Tamar without asking her father to leave work for a week to make the trip. Now that she knew the truth of her aunt's journey, she knew it was only a matter of time before her father mentioned that he did not want to see what happened to Aunt Yael happen to her.

"Matthew," Katya said, "she is our daughter. She is our only daughter. I treasure her in ways that only you and I can understand."

"I do not want to lose her," Matthew answered. "However, she makes a reasonable argument. She has made this trip alone, and she does know the way, but I do not like the idea. How will we ever know if she made it there safely or that we need to go looking for her?"

"Matthew, she knows what happened to Yael now. I told her everything, now that she is becoming a woman. At this time of the year, there is a need to have you home, and you can go and bring her home the next time you and Effron head to the coast to trade." Matthew and Katya had already talked in private, but Katya needed to say this again with her daughter listening.

Matthew positioned himself in front of his only daughter. He put his hands on her shoulders and looked her in the eye. "No normal Jewish man would entertain such a foolish conversation as this. Your purity and your well-being are my responsibility. Your safety lies upon us all to keep and maintain. You are no exception to Hebrew tradition nor the laws under which we all must live."

He pulled his hands off of her face and held her hands. He took a deep breath and kissed her on the forehead in the same way that he kissed Katya. "However, the world is different, and I agree that you would not be any safer traveling with anyone else from our village. Our horses can outrun the Roman ones, and you know the way. Come, Eliza, receive a blessing."

There was no defense against a father's love and words spoken in love. He reached up to wipe away a single tear that fell from her eye, but she turned her head away from him, feeling shame for shedding tears for him to see. He was, after all, the greatest man in her life. She desired to appear brave and strong before him, and her tears did not help her achieve that outcome.

Matthew motioned to her to kneel in front of him. She placed her hands underneath his upper leg as he sat cross-legged, as was the Hebrew tradition. She closed her eyes and leaned back. Her father closed his eyes and raised his hands to heaven. He then spoke a prayer from his heart. "Yeshua, our Messiah, please send Your spirit of protection and take care of our daughter as she crosses Your holy land to reach her school many days distant. May the roads be free of crime and may her eyes, ears, and mind be fast to discern any dangers that come upon her. I beg for her protection in the name of the shed blood of Yeshua. Amen."

They all stood up, and Matthew would not let Eliza leave without one more message. "I know that you feel more alive when you are experiencing new things. Remember, my daughter, you are never alone. Keep the words taught to you by your uncle and aunt as close to your heart as you can. When all light fails, Jehovah Jireh will be there. He will provide for you the courage you did not think you have."

"Yes, Father," was all Eliza could say before her voice cracked.

"You shall leave on the morrow, right after breakfast. Make sure that you get all your provisions packed and your horse fed and groomed. Get Ishmael to look over the horse's shoes, bridle, and saddle before you leave. I want you to make sure that all things are in the best of order." With that, Matthew left to visit some of the village leadership to discuss what he had decided. They promised to be home before they went to bed.

Eliza was overjoyed, and she hugged her mother as soon as her father had left. She could not wait to tell Aunt Yael about all of her exploits traveling by herself once she reached Tamar. For a Hebrew girl in the time of emperor Titus, this moment was as magical as seeing your first rainbow.

MORE FORGETTABLE STORIES

Caleb was of age to have an obligation to listen to the men who came to see his parents. Just like many who had come before them, they told stories of miraculous events that they witnessed. There were tales of a dead man who was brought back to life and another of a pond used for irrigation that was completely refilled in the middle of the dry season. Caleb had seen some of these events with his own eyes, so he knew that they were real. Since his parents were celebrities in the growing Yeshuaian faith, it seemed like a grand story was an admission ticket to his family's house for dinner.

But he could never tell his parents that he wished he could stay during the part of the evening when they told their stories. Caleb found that there were always a few guests who loved hunting and fishing as he did, and they would tell him of great places to stalk game, sometimes with the same passion that they had for the tales of how Yeshua moved mountains. They were his favorite kinds of guests. Fortunately, his father took all the great maps from the Temple with him, and they were now kept in their synagogue. When guests would tell him of the best places to hunt, he would often get them to walk back to the synagogue with him the next morning and show him on the maps where game from their locality would travel during different seasons. He wrote codes on the Temple maps using both numbers and letters, so he could use them in the future if he ever reached their part of the empire.

"Young Caleb, there is much you must know to understand our faith," said the leader of the guests on this particular night. "We want to invite you to visit us and our church one day in Antioch. Perhaps we can go hunting while you are there."

He had received invitations to visit these newer Yeshua-based synagogues many times. However, since this man mentioned hunting, Caleb decided that one day he would go to Antioch. Perhaps he would even visit the synagogue as well.

"To begin, we heard you referring to us as members of The Way. We are called 'Yeshuaians' now or 'Yeshua Followers,'" this man said.

"Yes, sir," Caleb replied. Caleb readily allowed himself to be corrected by those who he respected. In his mind, anyone who proclaimed that they hunted was a respectable man.

"We are the men and women from Jerusalem who saw with our own eyes the fall of the Temple, just as was predicted in the ancient scrolls by the prophet Isaiah. Once the Temple crumbled, we knew that God had changed His appearance to us on the earth. His character, His love, and His permanence did not change, but through the presentation of His Son and our Messiah, we are now different in action and in faith."

For a seemingly unending period of time, these men told stories of the events from Antioch. There were tales of a woman being raised from the dead. There was a story of three young boys who turned rocks into bread while they were lost in a cave; when the boys were found a week later, there were three loaves in the cave with them, still warm. The only story that made an impression on Caleb was a tale of a time when everyone in Antioch had the same dream of three men riding into their village on horses. The same evening, three men rode into the village on horses, all weeping. The leaders of Antioch approached the men, telling them they had been expecting their arrival. The men dismounted their horses and were led to the center of Antioch, and different members of the village began telling them of their dreams the night before.

People from all over both Judah and occasionally from as far as Rome would come to read the writings that Caleb's parents stored in the vaults, including the original scrolls from the Second Temple that Mishi saved. Last month, scribes from both Thessalonica and Cyprus had come to make copies of those scrolls to take back to their churches and schools. Caleb's parents had also accumulated writings from Yeshua's brother James from Rufus. There were two scrolls from the Yeshuaian teacher Paul. His stories were important, as they came from Rome and were the most talked about of all the writings in their vault. To Caleb, the inside of their synagogue was more a library than a synagogue.

It was already early winter, and it was the end of the day, both of which made for ideal hunting conditions. The heart of winter was now upon them, and the Romans imposed an extra tax on everyone for hunting during that season, as revenue was no longer coming from the harvest. Every minute Caleb spent listening to these tales meant one less minute tracking game. He rocked back and forth in his seat, making it clear he was ready to leave.

As the men got up to retire for the evening, Mishi turned to his son and said something that he knew would be more interesting to him. "It is near time to begin another session of school. Although I haven't received any word yet, I would expect your family from Correae to be arriving soon. That means you can take your cousin hunting with you again."

"Really? That's great! You know, Father, Eliza hates hunting. Uncle Matthew, though, he likes it!"

Neither of them had any idea Eliza would be coming alone.

ELIZA TRAVELS TO TAMAR

Eliza ate her breakfast quickly and helped her mother only to the extent that she needed help. Katya saw that her interest was elsewhere and let her out of some of her chores so she could depart. Eliza did not need much time to get ready, as she had made all the necessary arrangements the afternoon before once she had received her father's blessings. She only needed to wait for the bread to finish cooking and make a short trip to the river to fill her two waterskins.

She told her parents that she would reach Tamar late on the third day. Her horse allowed her to cut her travel time in half as long as the paths were open. She would stay at safe houses where former students of her aunt and uncle now lead a new Yeshuaian gathering, and she would use main roads the first two days. She would leave Roman roads on the last day and instead cross through two different forested sections to reach some remote roads south of Jerusalem that avoided Roman encampments between Jerusalem and the sea. Those encampments were places where bad things happened to Hebrews with no accountability for the perpetrator.

Her father had a great sense of direction, even though he had only visited Jerusalem once, and he made her recall the route she would take west of the City of David, making sure she would avoid Roman training camps. He also asked her where she would stop and let her horse drink while she rested. Once she answered the last question, he shooed her away, as one might shoo away a fly on his dinner plate. She knew he was being playful, and she stepped up to him, kissed him on the cheek, and said, "Goodbye, Daddy." Then, she walked towards her horse to leave on her journey.

But she was stopped immediately as some of the village elders approached her. "Please, we must talk to you. Before you leave your home, it is important you understand that you are carrying the fate of all of us with you."

Eliza knew to listen; her father always showed great respect for these men, and she would do the same. She assumed she would only be warned of dangers along the way, no different than what her parents had already told her. They stood around her in a circle, and her parents joined. From their body language, it was obvious that her parents knew the words about to be shared. The mayor was there, and he spoke first.

"Normally, this job is one that your father must do as the assimilator in our village of new residents. However, the village has decided that I shall do it. This message is too important to leave to chance or misunderstanding."

Eliza was concerned, and she looked at her father for validation.

"It is okay, Little One," he assured her. "This is important and requires great courage. I am sure you can do this."

She returned her gaze to the elder as he began. "Our village's success is built around our great wealth and our secret of gold. In the event that you are taken by the Romans or other angry factions of Jews, you must let that secret die with you. You do not have permission to share the secret of our wealth, even if it means you give your life. Our village is more important than anyone's life. You must understand and embrace the writing of Paul when he says that you are to offer your body as a living sacrifice, holy and pleasing to God." The mayor waited for her to acknowledge what he had said.

"I understand," she said, which was all she could muster. "So, are you expecting me to kill myself if I am caught?"

"Of course not!" said the elders, almost in unison. "The opposite is true. You must fight and try to escape at every chance, even if it means dying. Defending yourself is acceptable. There are many stories in the Old Testament of Hebrews killing their oppressors."

Eliza let out a sigh of relief.

"Since you are carrying a great deal of gold," the mayor went out, "you will need an alibi to explain where it came from." With that, one of the elders gave her a bill of sale and a large pot of frankincense to show where her current wealth came from. He instructed her to tell anyone that she intended to barter gold for another's harvest. He instructed her to carry the gold on her in several different places. She wanted to tell them that she already knew this strategy and was going to show them her three leather pouches where she carried her coins, but she wanted to just leave. She nodded in agreement and bit her tongue instead.

When the mayor was done, her mother put a hand on her shoulder.

"We have learned a great deal about Yahweh's heart in these last years since the Messiah came to earth. We have been taught how to use the gift of the Holy Spirit that Yeshua gave us before He left. This is one of those moments where we will call upon His power."

Each person placed one hand on her shoulder and on each other, and her father began to pray. As her father and head of their household, it was Matthew's responsibility to be the spiritual leader. Katya loved him in this role.

"Father, You told the Levites to lay hands. You told Moses to lay hands. You told your apostle Paul to kindle afresh the gift of laying of hands. As Your prophet Luke shared with my sister and brother-in-law, You desire us to come to You and ask You for Your touch. We pray for the Holy Spirit to send His anointing on my daughter as she begins a journey away from our protection. We live in trying times, as have our ancestors before. We thank You, in advance, for the power of Yeshua protecting our daughter as she crosses the remnants of the Promised Land."

He leaned forward and kissed his daughter on the forehead, and the elders started humming, chanting something that Eliza could not understand. She began to sob, even though she did not know why.

Her mother spoke. "Great Yahweh, bless our daughter. Cover her in Your protection as she travels into what used to be Your lands but is now the lands of the enemy. Keep her safe. Keep her eyes sharp and her mind alert. Let her see the path before with clarity that the world cannot understand. Treat her as Your precious daughter, just as her father and I do."

Prior to Yael becoming a rabbi, it was unheard of for a woman to lead a prayer that included village elders present. Truly, the world was changing. Even though Katya was no rabbi, she was now entrusted to lead public prayer as her sister had paved the way for this to be spiritually acceptable.

A smile appeared on Eliza's face. She wanted to speak and thank her mother for these last days, but she did not know what to say or how to express her gratitude.

The elders stopped chanting, and everyone took turns embracing Eliza. The mayor reached into his tunic and took out a small purse of leather, tied with a string. "Normally, the eldest person from the village pays for rabbinical services for the education of its youth. This transaction is hidden from the students. Since you have excellent intuition with all financial dealings, we permanently extend this task to you. Take this purse and give it to your uncle after you are settled into their home. It contains half a talent for your education for the next four cycles and an additional talent as a donation to their charity work. Until you arrive, do not take it out. In fact, keep these gold coins out of sight from anyone you meet. We stamped them as they came from our kiln with a Roman inscription like others we have found, so no one can trace them back to our village. However, this is enough gold to justify killing you and leaving you on the side of the road." They handed her the bag, and she was amazed at how heavy it was. These were real golden coins without any impurities, most likely smelted yesterday.

"And this is also for you." He handed her another allotment of coins, including copper, gold, and most precious silver. It was meant to be spent while she was on the road to Tamar, as well as in the town during the school session. Although this purse was smaller, it reinforced the importance that the village placed on tithing to those that serve the Lord. After all, what she needed was less important than what her aunt and uncle needed.

And with that, Eliza mounted her horse, telling it to begin a trot out of town on the only road out.

"See you soon!" her mother yelled as she departed.

Little did Eliza know that her parents would be half a day behind her.

A Difficult Family Reunion

Eliza arrived in Tamar without incident. Each of the church communities she stayed with on the previous two nights had been welcoming. As instructed, she arrived at the very end of each day, a few moments before sunset, as she did not want to draw any attention to her arrival or departure. Each place she visited provided for her needs, and she never needed to use any of her provisions either for dinner or for breakfast. Her horse always received grooming services and all the fodder it could eat. She had perfect weather, never needing her heavy cloak for warmth nor her deer hide for rain protection.

In her mind, the best part for her was that she did not spend a coin. Eliza loved managing finances and found pride in keeping her spending reigned in. She felt pride as she rode her horse in the wilderness between villages, knowing that her village leaders had entrusted her with managing some of the finances. Perhaps one day, she would become the village treasurer.

On her trip through the forested region, she decided to give the two different sections names. She called one section "the North Forest." The second forest was "the South Forest," and although it was smaller, it always seemed to have more wildlife. This trip was no exception, as there was a fox carrying a recently killed rabbit in its mouth, not even a stone's throw in front of her when she first entered.

It was the lack of incident that was the worst part of the trip for her. She had to admit to herself as she neared Tamar that she had hoped for more adventure, but there was nothing of significance to talk about. Long before sunset on the third day, she found herself in sight of the arched entrance into Tamar, where both her aunt and uncle's home and her school were located.

As her horse arrived at the hamlet, she went directly to the school, bypassing her parent's orders of going to her aunt and uncle's house. She found the school full of activity, as school was scheduled to start two days after the following Sabbath. She saw many of her friends doing the same thing she was, checking in and confirming the start in a few days. Village volunteers were readying the school grounds, making it look beautiful. Firewood was being delivered and stacked outside both the boys' and the girls' dorms, and a wagon full of grains, oils, and lentils had already been delivered. Enrollment at the school was now nearly as great as the village's entire population, and some builders and Roman administrators from the coast had come to survey where the next buildings would be placed. Last year's farming expectations were met, and both slaves and citizens were moving the last of the extra wheat straw into a large mud house for storage for the wet and cold winter months ahead. Some flowers had been planted outside the window in the office where the rabbis worked. There was also new thatched reed grass on the roof to keep the facility waterproof during the rainy season and cool during the hot season. The school looked nearly ready.

Before she took even ten steps onto the school's grounds, she was knocked to the ground. She looked up to see her cousin, Caleb. He laughed and apologized in complete insincerity.

"You donkey! That wasn't an accident! Why did you do that?"

Her words only made him laugh harder, "Hey, Eliza. How've you been? And where is everybody? Where are your mom and dad? You did not come here, alone, did you? I want to go hunting with Uncle Matthew."

Here was her first big chance to brag about coming alone. "You are looking my entire entourage!"

"Wow," he said. "Your parents let you come here alone?"

He was obviously jealous, and that made her day. He knew the hills and caves of the area better than nearly anyone, but he never had permission to travel overnight by himself. He was the son of two Jewish rabbis, a most unique status in the history of all of Judah, and he knew he would never get his parent's approval to do such a thing until Yeshua returned to rule forever and ever.

Eliza smiled and put her hand on her hips. She loved the satisfaction of doing something her cousin could not do. He had always been bigger, faster, and stronger than she was, even though the two of them were born only days apart. It made her effort to convince her parents to let her travel alone worthwhile. They joked a lot, as teenagers do, and the two of them sat down as Eliza shared every boring detail that she could remember from the journey. The only time Caleb really paid attention was when she talked about the fox and rabbit she saw on the way, asking her lots of questions about the size of the fox and whether or not the rabbit was still moving. Eliza did not really care about that, and both got bored pretty quickly.

She heard her aunt's voice coming from their home, and she stood up and ran towards her, breaking off the conversation with Caleb abruptly. She and her aunt embraced as only two Jewish women could. This was the first school session since the break for harvest, and the two of them missed each other.

"Oh my, you have grown up, my dear. You are most certainly looking like a woman, and, of course, more and more like your mother...and me!"

They both laughed and hugged again. But it was the first moment Eliza felt it to be a bit troubling that Caleb and she did not look that much alike.

"Eliza, would you like to help me make dinner?"

"Auntie, I brought some of Correae's olive oil with me. I want to use that. Is that okay?"

"Yes! Yes! Let's use that."

They went back to their house and began dinner preparations. Yael and Eliza had a lot to catch up on. Caleb ran off to play with his friends.

"Auntie, can I ask you some questions?" Eliza said as they settled into their normal routine in the kitchen, with her two slaves assisting her in the readying of all the materials.

"Of course." Yael could sense what was coming.

"Mom told me about how you left Correae to travel to Jerusalem for redemption. Part of that story I had heard before, but I did not know about why you left until a few days ago."

Yael smiled. She knew this day would come, and she knew to let her older sister initiate the conversation.

"In our culture, we teach young men and women the importance of purity before marriage. I tested those boundaries with a young man who I did not know, thinking he would be special to me one day. He never had any intention

56

of that outcome. I made two mistakes that day. I decided to ignore the teachings of God, and I decided to trust that boy. The first one was my mistake. The second one is a natural error that anyone can make. God forgave me for the first one, and I forgave myself for the second one."

Eliza could only listen. Now that she was a woman, she no longer looked at boys as stupid rats, as she used to. Had she heard this story last year, she would not have understood it. Now that she was of childbearing age, thoughts of what her husband would be like appeared in her mind on occasion, and she liked talking about them with her aunt.

"We learned from our dear friend Paul when we were in Rome before you were born that God uses all things to bring Himself glory. I told Paul my story, and he laughed! Do you know what he said? He said he used to kill Jews, and now God had used him to teach others how to save themselves for eternity. I gave up my body only to see God use it to record the words of one of His disciples. It seems like God has a sense of humor in how He has used both of us."

Eliza started laughing as she had heard tales of Paul repeatedly.

"Oh, I was not expecting him to talk like that to me, that is for sure," Yael said.

Yael looked at the ceiling wistfully. "Paul was a servant of God. I loved that man. It made me sad when he died, but we all must die, you know? What better of a thing to do than die trying to save your friends? That is what he said. He was teaching the prison guards the morning he was killed. Did you know that?"

"I did not." Eliza hesitated, but she decided to say what was burning on the tip of her tongue.

"Mom also told me that you were raped by a Roman soldier and that Caleb came from that."

"Yes, this is true, as well."

Eliza began to cry again. She hated crying in front of her aunt, as she really wanted to prove herself to be a strong woman when she was in Yael's presence. Tears seemed to make her feel like a failure.

"Mom said that I must not treat Caleb any differently than before I knew this. She said Caleb is an heir to God's kingdom like any Jew born of blood."

"Your mother understands the message of the Messiah, Little One. Yeshua did not come for the Jews. He came for everyone who sins. Which is everybody!" Yael paused to wipe the tears from Eliza's eyes, even though both of them were laughing again.

"I hate this crying! I did it before I left to come here, too!" said Eliza. Yael drew her into her chest and held her head while rubbing it.

"The best part of the message of Yeshua in our family has been your uncle's demonstration of his love towards me and Caleb. Your uncle has given every moment of time and every extra coin he has to raising and loving Caleb as if he were his own blood and flesh. Caleb feels this love, and the two of them love each other. But sometimes, it is obvious that they aren't of the same blood. Caleb is very strong and fast, and my Mishi is not!" That got a big laugh from everyone, including the two slaves helping them in the kitchen with food preparation.

Yael told stories of Caleb's physical prowess. She loved how he could run fast one minute and carry such heavy loads the next. Caleb had been a hunter of great skill for many years, but lately, he seemed even better than before. He would tell her that sometimes he gave the meat away from his kills to travelers who looked to be in need. "I think he learned the skill of protecting and sharing with those who are less fortunate from his father. Both of them have big hearts like that," she added. "Now that he has transitioned into becoming a man, I am glad that he hunts game instead of women."

Both of them began laughing again.

"Auntie, I love you. You know, you are my hero. When I was traveling here alone on my horse these last three days, I thought about what it must have been like for you the first time you left Correae to travel alone to Jerusalem," Eliza said.

Yael wiped another tear from Eliza's eye. Her crying showed no signs of abetting.

"That was a crazy story, about how Yahweh used that hurtful experience to bring great good to the world. Now we are done talking about the men in our lives today, okay? It is time to feed them!"

As dinner neared, Yael went outside and called for Caleb. He was hungry and arrived quickly, sneaking a piece of bread from the oven before his father entered and blessed the meal. They all sat and ate together. As dinner was winding down, Mishi spoke up for the first time that evening since blessing the meal. Caleb was already on his third portion of bread and hummus while the women talked incessantly, barely eating their food. "Yael, let the slaves take care of all the cleaning. It is time to talk to our son about his past. Since Eliza arrived here by herself, I believe she is old enough to hear this story. Caleb will need her support. She is his family."

Mishi turned to Caleb. "Young man, come sit next to me. This story requires that you be next to me."

Caleb did not hesitate. That left Eliza sitting next to her aunt. With that shifting of seats complete, Mishi began. "My son, you have heard how I met your mother in an abandoned tunnel left behind from the days of King David underneath the city of Jerusalem many years ago. Neither of us was much older than the two of you are now. You have also heard how we were moved by the Holy Spirit and helped Luke record the words spoken to him and given to him by Yahweh Himself. It is the content of those stories that brings people from synagogues all over the Roman Empire to us. What I did not tell you is an important piece of information regarding how you came to be my son."

Caleb looked perplexed. "What? What do you mean, Father?"

His father had taken him into the wilderness just this year and explained to him God's plan for procreation and how that plan works. One man and one woman come together, and through this union, children are created. It is an act of love that occurs once a Jewish man leaves his parents' home and builds a home for himself and his bride. Then, and only then, do they sleep together and create offspring.

"You know that I met your mother in Jerusalem. What you do not know is that she came to Jerusalem to atone for a sin she had done a year earlier that she hid from everyone."

Caleb looked at his mother. "Mother, what sin?"

Yael began to look pale, and she reached out and put her arm around Eliza. "Keep listening to your father."

Eliza noticed her aunt's tear as she spoke, and her view of her aunt forever changed in that moment. Her aunt did not look the part of a great teacher and the leader of a movement of strong Yeshuaian women. She was no longer a teacher of the sacred scrolls, revered for her insight in how to read and write many languages. She was now a teenage girl who had never healed from a hurt from half a lifetime ago. Instead, this great woman now looked frail and weak, ready to begin sobbing.

"Your mother had sexual relations with a boy who was temporarily staying in Correae, and the guilt it caused made her suffer. She left to come to Jerusalem to sacrifice at the altar in the Temple to atone for her sin, as was the Jewish custom."

Caleb looked at his mother with his mouth wide open. "Really, mother?" he rhetorically asked.

"Yes, my son. That is what happened to me. That is what I did," she said, making sure to point out and separate both her choice and its impact.

"After your mother and I met, she secretly left the great city to find a suitable sacrifice so I could lead her through our ritual of forgiveness of sin. After she slipped through the tunnels under the city, she found herself on the fields in front of the city. She was raped by a Roman soldier and became pregnant. Son, you are biologically the son of a Roman soldier."

Before Caleb could speak and attempt to unwind the mystery just revealed, Yael began to talk to her son with a cracking in her voice that neither Eliza nor Caleb had ever heard. "When I was falling in love with your father, I worked with him nearly every day to record the words of our teacher Luke. I did not know I was with a child! We were consumed by the task in front of us of recording the word of God, and we spent nearly every moment together, taking turns writing the words Luke spoke to us. It did not register in my mind that I missed my menses. Your father was far from his family, and I had left Correae with only my father aware of my choice to travel to Jerusalem alone."

Both children were speechless. Eliza had only been given the high points of the story. She did not know these details. And it was unheard of women to speak about their monthly cycle in the presence of men. Mishi again spoke.

"I was already falling in love with your mother before I learned that she was with another man's child," he said. "At the same time, I was learning from Luke that our Messiah was conceived by someone who was also not His earthly father."

Mishi gestured for his cup to be filled with some red wine. The children only saw him do this on special occasions. "As we are taught, Mary's soon-to-be husband had the choice to leave her, without disgrace, once he learned that she was carrying someone else's child. He could also have chosen to have her stoned to death. Rabbi Luke told me that Yeshua forgave all of us for our sins from the past. In exchange, the Messiah asked us to follow Him."

"So, you married Aunt Yael, knowing that she was with child from another man?" asked Eliza.

"Yes, Little One, I did. It was the best decision I have ever made."

Yael had been holding her niece closely, resting her head on the thirteen-year-old's shoulder, caressing her dark brown hair. Yael was now lightly weeping, as were both the slaves.

Mishi smiled at his wife before returning his gaze to his son. "Caleb, this event does not change the legitimacy of the love your mother and I have for you. You are our son, and we have raised you to be both a Hebrew and a Yeshuaian. Although none here will ever know your biological father's name, I am your father on earth, as Yahweh is your Father in heaven. Your mother and I believe that you need nothing else. You need no one else, perhaps other than a wife of your own one day."

Caleb was thoughtfully silent, but Eliza was bursting with questions. "Aunt Yael, how did all that happen? With the Roman, I mean."

Yael told the story as best as she could, of seeing her first Behemoth outside the city walls and being sexually assaulted by the man overseeing the beasts. She talked of shame, but she also talked of what she learned. "Romans not only make slaves of Jews, but they make slaves of themselves. They follow the emperor, and they fear him more than we do. They fear that they will be humiliated, that their family will be banished and perhaps even killed. As Yeshuaians, we are commanded not to have that same fear. No matter what happens to our bodies on earth, we will see our Savior in heaven one day. Our brother John received a vision from the Messiah Himself, telling us that we once again will have a New Jerusalem, far bigger and grander than the one that your father and I knew. This is the hope that allows me to continue. I still carry this hope with me, even now as I talk to you. Above all other children, I love the two of you the most of any in this world."

Yael paused as she once again had the aura of a polished and courageous speaker, capable of commanding an audience with only the authority of her voice and the authenticity of her tales. "There can be no doubt as I replay these events of my life that God's word is true. He uses all things for His glory, including my rape and Caleb's birth. The very day that I was raped, the Romans sieged the city, and eventually, they destroyed it. Words cannot describe the despair I felt that day. God provided and answered my prayers, even before I spoke them. I met an old woman who you have heard me talk about, who helped guide me to meet the early Yeshuaians. Had I found a sacrificial animal and proceeded to get your father to perform the ritual of atonement, I would most likely have secretly left Jerusalem and returned to Correae, never meeting Luke, your uncle Rufus, or any of the Yeshuaians. I would not have become a rabbi. I would not have found a man who I could marry and be completely honest with, and perhaps I would still be living in shame at my father and mother's home in Correae, as no Jew could ever marry a soiled woman. God has protected me from this outcome."

She paused before continuing, making eye contact with all three of her family.

"Look at us now. We have been given the gift to teach others for the remainder of our days and raise our son to be a man. I could not possibly have had a better outcome; I tell you the truth."

"Son," Mishi said, "when your mother and I discussed telling you this tale, she did not want you to think of her as a victim or me as a heroic rescuer. Others have tried to portray us in these roles, and these depictions are not right. You, my son, not only filled our lives with joy and restored hope, but your presence in our lives has also healed both of us. In the same way your mother was a sinner and needed atonement, I, too, was a sinner. I have not told you this story, but I was hiding rations and supplies under the old Temple so that I could survive by myself after the Romans sacked the city. All the while, I watched men, women, and some young children starve to death. I had food to share with them, but I did not. Had your mother not left hastily, I would have survived under the city for half a year, long enough to avoid Roman scrutiny, and I would never have met Luke, Rufus, or any of the people you now see coming to our house."

"Why are you now telling us this?" asked Caleb.

Mishi looked at his wife, and she answered for him. "Some people have been told the story that you have just heard in a milder version in the synagogues and towns around us. We did not want you to hear this story from someone else, as this is a story about you and your past. You needed to hear it from us. Now, you both know why you are much taller and stronger than I am!"

This comment broke the tension in the room, and everyone began to laugh. Both parents got up and approached their son, embracing him like he was a newborn baby. He loved the affection and smiled broadly.

"And, since Eliza is now traveling alone, we have decided that you can do the same."

Caleb's eyes widened. "Really?"

Mishi grabbed his son with one hand on each side of his head. "You are ours, and you are Yeshua's, all at the same time. If you can track and hunt wild animals, you can travel the roads of Judah and explore creation without any limits that we will place on you. God has already done great things with you, and I am assured that you will yet do great things for Him!"

After all of them stood up, Eliza wrapped her arms around Caleb and cried for what she hoped was the last time today. "Cousin, my love for you has grown greatly this evening. Consider me part of your faithful family for all times." He leaned over and kissed her head. Mishi took that moment to embrace his wife and kiss her as well.

"So...when can I start traveling alone?" Caleb said.

Both parents and cousin chuckled.

"Your mother and I would prefer it if you two could do it together this first time. The school has been delayed for a few days, as the Romans need to inspect the grounds. You can go as soon as tomorrow if you like."

Not a Typical First Adventure

The next morning, after breakfast was done and the slaves had begun cleaning up, Caleb asked Eliza to help him make his provisions for winter travel. She took her uncle's backpack and put a bedroll on the bottom of it, wrapped in a deerskin to keep dry. She put a tinder kit along with some flint in a small satchel and attached it with some leather straps next to the wooden pack frame. She took two of her aunt's old water skins and filled them, attaching them to the top of the pack.

"Put this on, so you can feel how much this weighs and get used to it."

Caleb put the pack on and adjusted the straps on each side to get the most comfortable fit he could. He quickly took the pack off and opened the top up. "I need to add the good stuff, now," he said, and he came back with his sling, his short bow, a quiver of arrows, his stones, two knives, and two metal cups and bowls. "Now, that will give me what we need to eat," he said with a lot of pride.

Eliza rolled her eyes and put her hands on her hips. Then, she spoke, sounding a lot like her mother. "You know, there are cutlery and plates at the inns around Judah." She added some items from the kitchen, including salt, spices, dried meat, and warm bread.

Caleb pointed to the dry meat. "We will never need it. We will eat fresh meat. God will provide."

Eliza was quick to respond. "But you might not provide. That is why we have your mom's food."

Caleb stuck his tongue out at her, and they both laughed.

The two of them selected Kedron, on the river Gath, in ancient Philistia, to be their first foreign land they would visit together. They told Caleb's parents and finished their preparations. The Philistines were as much overrun with Rome's heavy-handed rule as Judah. Caleb's parents repeatedly warned them about approaching groups of Philistine men or groups of Roman soldiers who looked bored. Mishi told them what to look for and how to speak to Roman militia if they had an encounter. He helped them practice speaking slang Greek of the sort that all Roman soldiers would understand. He also taught him hand gestures and told them only to use them if the situation required it.

Eliza gave her uncle the tithe coins from her village but kept the education coins. Those would go to the school once classes commenced. He accepted them and put them on the top of the small wall in the kitchen. He reached inside and gave four coins to each of the slaves, instructing them to give them to the rabbi in charge at the school to pay for their children's education this session. All were speechless except Yael.

"Husband, you are a man after Yeshua's heart, aren't you?" she said, kissing him on the lips without embarrassment. Neither Caleb nor Eliza responded to this display of affection, as it was allowed inside of one's home. However, the slaves were overcome with gratitude, and they both placed their hands in a prayerlike position and thanked Mishi for the gift.

The trip to Kedron was fast and easy. Eliza rode on her horse, going slower than she otherwise would since her cousin was walking and running next to her. She repeatedly asked Caleb if he wanted to put his pack on the horse, but he always said no, thinking he needed the exercise. As they reached the outskirts of Kedron near the river, he spotted three deer.

He grabbed the horse's reigns and gestured to Eliza to cease any conversation. She nodded, already feeling the excitement of the hunt that was about to happen. She slowly stepped off the horse, and Caleb reached in his pack for his bow and quiver of arrows. He stayed low to the ground, notched a single arrow, and began to stalk the deer.

From experience, Eliza knew that this could take considerable time, and there was a real chance he would come back with nothing but a bad attitude. She reached for a water skin and took a deep drink while her cousin left her field of vision. She decided to sit and wait for her cousin while she prayed for his success.

Before she could finish even a quarter of water left in her skin, she heard Caleb calling her. She mounted her horse and quickly crossed the hill that separated them. Caleb was on one knee, already bleeding the deer.

"She had no idea I was coming. She should have. The shadow of the afternoon sun should have given me away. Stupid animal forgot to use her eyes." He made another cut in her abdomen, pulling out the entrails.

"Do you have to do that now?" Eliza commented with disgust.

Caleb did not have any interest in responding.

"It sure did not hurt that I was a good shot! This deer will provide us fresh meat and a reason to go to the market to sell the rest, Eliza." He lifted up his arrow and showed it to her. "This arrow has already killed three deer this season. It's my favorite."

And the idea to enter a marketplace with something to sell was Eliza's love language. That promise helped her set aside any repulsion she was experiencing. Many of the boys in her village would go out hunting, but few succeeded this quickly. That deserved some acknowledgment, but she did not want it to go to his head, so she said nothing. Deep down, though, she was impressed.

"Let's take this to Kedron right now!" He pointed to the city ramparts, less than a league away. "We can sell most of this meat, as the markets will still be open, and this time of day, fresh game sells at a premium." He hoisted the deer onto his shoulders after all the bleedings were complete and began walking.

"What about your stuff?" Eliza asked.

"Oh, would you mind getting all of that for me? This animal is heavy." She shook her head as he slung the dead animal over his shoulders and began walking to the city walls. She knew that animal weighed nearly as much as he did, so she picked up the pack, attached it to their horse, and began following him towards the city walls.

As he predicted, Eliza all but ignored him once they entered the market. Caleb was merely the meat-carrying guy. She negotiated great prices for fresh deer, as it could be stored outside for much of the remainder of winter. They left the market after selling the deer to two different butchers who treasured different cuts of the animal. They left with several coins of various types, all legal tender in Roman-occupied lands. Caleb and Eliza were happy with their efforts, but it was also time to arrange their evening accommodations. Neither of them had been to this city before, so the act of selecting an inn and ordering dinner would be new to both of them.

They negotiated a room at the inn near the local synagogue and found that the manager of the inn was a Yeshuaian. Thinking it was safe to speak freely, as there were no Romans present, Caleb engaged the innkeeper in a brief conversation about killing the deer and bringing it to be sold while the meat was still fresh. Eliza looked around at the other people in the inn's lobby, and she also felt a bit safer than she had expected. It was very much like her experience traveling to Tamar from Correae a few days earlier.

Caleb introduced her to the innkeeper. "This is my cousin, Eliza, from the village of Correae, far to the north. She attends school with me. We are traveling in the area, and we need a room for one night. Two beds, please."

Eliza smiled. She did not know if a truthful disclosure of their actual names was the right decision, but it was too late to undo it now. Caleb was always quicker to speak than to think.

When they woke up the next morning, the room was cold, as it was far from the fireplace that heated the structure. They did not pay the extra coin to have a room with a fireplace, as they each had carried a blanket from Caleb's home. Once they got up with the courage to stand up in the cold and get dressed, Eliza led the way out of the room and towards the banqueting partition of the inn. They ate a breakfast of fresh bread, hummus, and dried apples. They each drank two cups of hot tea mixed with camel milk and honey to warm them.

Caleb followed his cousin's lead. After washing their hands, feet, and faces, they retrieved Eliza's horse from the manger, giving the attendant a copper coin for his efforts.

Eliza mounted the horse, and Caleb walked next to her as they left the city.

Tamar was only a few hours away from Kedron. They sang school songs along the way, and they each offered up a prayer for the safety of the children and the school and that they have a powerful educational experience this session. When they crested the last hill before the plains surrounding Tamar, both of them stopped in their tracks. Although his family's village was small and still far away, they could see that some of the buildings near the center of the town were on fire, burning as if struck by lightning. The two teenagers felt disbelief.

"What did the Romans do?" Caleb asked rhetorically. For her part, Eliza remained paralyzed, unable either to move or to speak. Sounds carried well to the top of this hill. They heard shouting and saw some animals running outside of the village that should not have been there. Most of what they heard wasn't Hebrew but Greek. That meant Roman soldiers or marauders were down there.

"Something is really wrong," said Caleb in a quiet and calm voice. Eliza was about to yell out, but Caleb put his hand over her mouth and whispered. "Quiet! We must remain in control of our emotions. They do not know we are here or who we are, and we need to keep it that way. Tie the horse off and walk down there with me." *Giving her a specific task might calm her and engage her,* he thought.

He took out his bow and both knives and put his entire quiver of arrows on his back. He tightened his sandals and took a long drink of water before offering it to Eliza. She took a deep drink and set the water skin on the horse. "Just breathe and follow my lead. We have got to stay calm." Caleb took her hand, and they quickly went down the side of the hill.

They followed an animal trail into the village, staying off the main road. The animal trail provided tree cover for them as well as places to stop and reassess the situation. Caleb remained levelheaded, but Eliza found herself breathing rapidly, and occasionally, she felt panic. Each time this happened, Caleb would stop and hold her head and stare into her eyes, telling her to keep a cool head and not do anything to draw attention towards them. He spoke with authority but quietly.

"I trust in two things right now. I trust in my skills, and I trust the stories I have heard in my life of how the Messiah hears our prayers. I will do my job, and you should pray. Come on!"

"Caleb, I trust you," she said.

"Good. Let's keep moving. I have to try to stop this," he whispered. They kept moving towards the village.

As they neared the village, they paused behind the last large tree to keep them out of sight of the town's residents. What they saw was a horror, unlike anything either of them had ever seen.

There were several dying bodies, most of them still bleeding out, and there were nearly a dozen Roman soldiers bringing more villagers to the center of town where what appeared to be a centurion stood, holding a gladius of steel in his right hand.

The centurion spoke loudly as four villagers we brought to him. "Is it true that the school you are about to open teaches that there is another, all-powerful God besides the emperor?"

The villagers did not answer his question. The penalty for publicly denying worship was death, and worshipping another was deemed to be the same activity. Two of the women were crying hysterically. One older man was composed enough to answer them. "Please do not kill us. We are no threat to you or to the emperor. We are a small Hebrew village thousands of leagues from Rome."

The centurion thrust his sword through the guts of the man, ignoring his pleas.

Eliza vomited, and she wanted to cry out, but Caleb grabbed her, whispering, "If you make a sound, we die!" She spat out the vomit that remained in her throat, cleaning her face with her robe. She wondered if she knew that man or if his children went to school with her.

The centurion turned towards the other man in the lot. "You shall answer my question!" he yelled. The two remaining women fell to their knees and began pleading for mercy in Hebrew.

Caleb looked away from the gruesome scene, and his eyes found something even more frightening. Near the village well, he saw his aunt and uncle near a large cart. Katya was crying, and Matthew was battered, lying on the ground. Matthew appeared to be attempting to stand up.

"Look, Eliza! It's your parents. They must have come the day after you did to surprise us all! Stay here but take this knife to defend yourself. I'm going to free some of these people." He was about to step towards the village when he turned and spoke to Eliza again. "Keep the knife hidden and close to you until you can strike someone without having to extend your arm all the way. Let them get close before you strike. The blade is sharp and will penetrate any flesh in the body with little effort. You do not have to hit with all your strength. Just push and do not stop until it is all the way in. Once it's in them, leave it. Then, run to the horse and go home. Tell everyone what you saw."

Eliza had her wits about her now. She wiped the tears from her face and took a deep breath. She was traumatized, but she had a plan. "Caleb, we must pray first together! Remember what we were taught? 'Where two or more are gathered in my name, so there I will also be.'"

They took each other's hands and spoke the prayer that both of their parents learned from their parents. Caleb led it. "Yahweh, Lord Yeshua, thank You that You are in heaven. Your name is great. May Your heaven come to earth as it is with You now. Give us our daily bread and forgive us our debts as we forgive our debtors. Especially today, deliver us from this evil. Amen."

In that moment, Caleb looked like a soldier and a warrior to Eliza. When she spoke, she used the tone that her mother would use when her father would leave in the mornings. "Caleb, you are becoming a great man, and you are becoming a man of God. He will bless you this day. It is my prayer. Go, Cousin. Do what you need to save our people."

"Thank you," he said. Then he left, going to the side of the village where the soldiers were not looking. It was time to defend the people in his village.

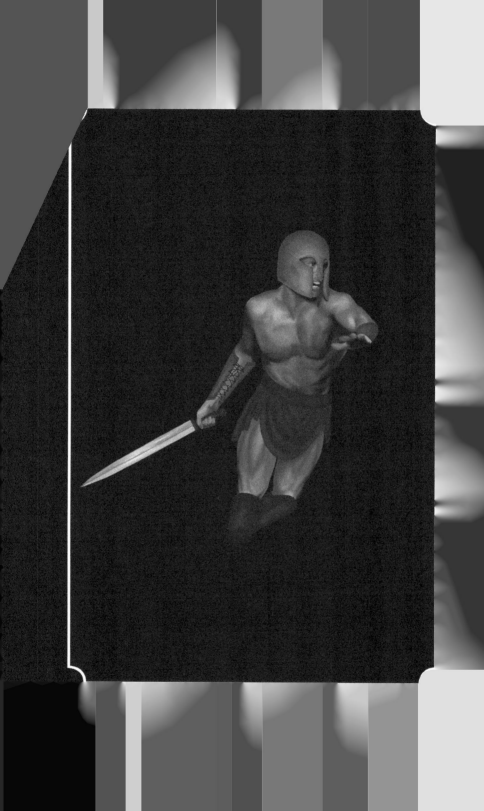

Mission Field at Home

Caleb circumnavigated all the houses on the edge of the village quickly and determined that there were eight Roman soldiers in the village worthy of his attention and training. The centurion with the steel gladius was the leader, as he was giving orders to the other seven. It was only mid-day, and Caleb concluded that they were not drunk on wine. He couldn't tell if the centurion in charge was just angry or trying to command respect, but he yelled at everyone. Caleb continually looked at his aunt and uncle, hoping that he could make eye contact with Matthew. Other villagers saw him as he gestured to them to remain quiet as he readied his attack plan.

After he rounded the outside edge of the house closest to the center of the village, Caleb finally made eye contact with Matthew. He saw his uncle's eyes bulging as he recognized his nephew. Matthew shook his head, trying to prevent his nephew from taking an unnecessary risk, but Caleb already had a plan. Caleb raised a finger to his lips to tell his uncle to be silent. Matthew made no gesture acknowledging him but stopped looking at him and returned to holding his scared wife.

Rage boiled in Caleb's veins upon seeing his family members enslaved in chains, but Katya at least looked unharmed. He had heard stories of Romans destroying villages and enslaving the residents, but he had never thought that it might happen to his own family. He felt a deep desire for revenge, and he knew he could kill or wound several of the soldiers before they knew what had happened. Their leather armor looked too thin to stop his arrows, as he kept them sharp enough to penetrate a deer's hide. He decided that he was going to take out the leader and eliminate a few of the perimeter soldiers.

Next to the last house was a village stable where the livestock of visitors was kept during the night. Caleb moved behind the horse stalls, and he cocked an arrow. He knew there would be two soldiers in front of him, and he would be at their backs. With the focus his uncle taught him, he turned the corner and used the element of surprise. He launched his first arrow at a soldier into his upper back, directly into his heart. He reached into his quiver for the second arrow, knowing the other soldier would quickly turn to face the attack. He shot the second arrow into his neck, making the man stand upright but unable to speak for a few moments. Caleb stared the man in the eyes as he faced his attacker. Finally, the man fell to the ground without ever speaking.

He put his bow back over his shoulder as he surveyed the ground. Among the pile of corpses that the two soldiers had made lay his mother with no life left in her body. His father lay next to her, bleeding out from the gut but still alive. He saw Caleb and spoke to him with as much effort as he could muster.

"My son! These men are fools. They may take the lives of your mother and me, but do not let them take yours."

In front of his parents lay three dead Romans. Two looked just like the others in the town, but Caleb recognized the third. It was his uncle Rufus. Rufus still held a wooden rake in his hands and was wearing no armor, but his stomach had been cut open.

"Go tell the world the story of our Savior," Mishi said. "The Romans may take our lives, but they cannot take our souls from our destiny with Yahweh in eternity."

Caleb yelled out, "No!"

The centurion and the two soldiers had already turned their attention away from the two hysterical women and the old man and looked in the direction of where their comrades had just fallen down. They were moving Caleb's way.

Caleb hastily executed his plan. His uncle's body was closest, so he reached down, taking up his gladius. His uncle had taught him how to use this exact weapon when he was even younger, and its weight was ingrained into Caleb's fighting tactics. Rufus looked him in the eye and grunted something. Caleb couldn't make out the words as Rufus's diaphragm was destroyed, but he knew what his uncle meant. Caleb removed the ring from Rufus's left hand. Then, he took the gladius and pressed the sharp tip into his uncle's chest, giving Rufus the end that he sought.

When Caleb turned, he saw that the two Roman soldiers were upon him, but the weight of their armor made their reflexes slow. He jumped back over the pile of bodies, wielded his bow, and fired an arrow at the soldier closest to him. Neither soldier was expecting a fast response, as the Hebrews those Romans normally met were not militarily aggressive.

Caleb screamed and notched a second arrow. He shot the second soldier. Then, Mishi began coughing, and Caleb ran to his father's side.

Mishi spoke in Greek, as it was easier, and his breathing was now very labored. "Run!" he said. His voice was weak, and the coughing lifted his chest off the ground.

Caleb leaned over his dying father. "I will kill them like the deer I killed yesterday!" he vowed.

"Son, do not let them kill you or your cousin. She is your family now."

"I won't, Father," he said, as tears of rage rolled down his cheek.

"Do not let them take your hope!" With that, Mishi breathed his last. When Caleb saw his chest stop moving, he changed his focus. There were three remaining guards wielding swords, and two were nearly on top of him. He launched another arrow into the gut of the one closest, then he turned to circle around the outside of the stables. One of the remaining warriors stopped to help the injured soldier, and Caleb shouldered his bow to switch to the gladius.

The centurion was not as naïve as his men and could tell that Caleb was trained in the ways of combat. Caleb rounded the corner of the stable that he had hoped would give him an unobstructed view of the leader, but the centurion knew that Caleb would take this route, and he was upon Caleb. The centurion's sword was already moving to attempt to decapitate him.

Caleb raised the arm holding the gladius, but he could not get it up high enough. The force of the strike hit Caleb's blade and knocked it from his hands. All the years of fighting with dogs had taught him that once a dog has your arm in its bite, the best strategy is to let it go limp and maneuver your body to better attack back. As the blade struck him, he let his arm go limp, and he fell to the ground, rolling towards the centurion. Caleb was now on the ground, and the centurion was preparing to strike him from above when Caleb reached up into the top of his boot and withdrew his hunting knife. With his left arm stinging from the force of the impact, Caleb used his right arm to drive the knife into the exposed calf of the Centurion, enough to get to the bone. As the Centurion screamed, Caleb pulled the knife down the full length of the man's calf until he struck the top of his shoe. He pulled the knife out and rolled over two times, as he knew the centurion could now no longer walk any distance.

Caleb stood up and yelled at the centurion, "Why did you attack and kill these people? What did they do to you?" He made sure he used the slang Greek his parents had taught him. He knew that if he called the villagers "my people," it would only be a matter of time before the Romans determined who he was and began a manhunt throughout all of Judah looking for him. That is not what his father wanted. He knew that his only hope of protecting his cousin was remaining anonymous.

The centurion was enraged and attempted to step forward to get close enough to swing at Caleb. But Caleb knew this was coming. He allowed him to swing with what Caleb hoped would be his maximum effort. The man met his expectation, and the blade zoomed past Caleb at a very high speed.

As soon as the blade passed him, Caleb lunged and struck the centurion in the underarm of his exposed shoulder, knowing that this move would require the centurion to place all of his weight on his bleeding calf. The centurion cried out and focused all of his attention on removing the weight off his wounded leg.

Life was in slow motion for Caleb at that moment, and he moved without any emotion. As the centurion adjusted his body weight, Caleb calmly stepped forward and ran his hunting knife across the man's throat, opening it up.

The centurion was in shock, but he was not yet dead. He moved his right arm rapidly, and his elbow armor struck Caleb in the head, causing him to see bright stars. Stunned, Caleb stood motionless, attempting to keep his balance. He knew that he need not maintain any defensive skills, as the centurion's efforts to strike him would further open the wound in his neck, and the blood would already be uncontrollably flowing out. He would be dead within three breaths.

When Caleb recovered from the blow to his head, he heard his aunt and uncle yelling at him to beware of the other soldier who was now approaching him. Without a clear vision, he could not use his bow. With shooting pains in his forehead, Caleb was not ready to fight again. Yet, even as he prepared to run away, he remembered his father's last words. "Protect your cousin. She is your family now."

He turned and ran. The remaining soldier in full combat gear could not sprint as fast nor run as far as Caleb could. He made his way through the village center towards the tree on the outskirts of town where Eliza remained. Once he reached it, he stopped and tried to look her in the eyes. Blood was now coming from his head, and it looked messy.

Hidden from the remaining soldiers by the protection of the tree, she looked at him and said in a low tone, "Your face! You need healing!"

Caleb knew that. It hurt. He reached up and touched it. His forehead was a bloody mess, but his brow had kept most of the blood from running into his eyes. He peered around the corner. The remaining soldier was angrily yelling out, calling for others who must have been in the area that Caleb did not see.

"Caleb, I talked to my parents. I told them that we would come back for them."

"Good. But we cannot stay here. These men will tell others and hunt us down. We need to get out of here right now."

She grabbed his hand, and the two of them took off up the hill.

HOUSE OF HEALING

Part 1

"Good morning, son of Mishi and son of Yael."

Caleb saw two men standing in the light of the only window in the room, both wearing the clothing of a rabbi. They dressed up with all the Hebrew regalia and looked like his father did during the Passover meal. The bed he lay in was beautiful, covered in linens made from Egyptian cotton, and Eliza was sitting on the bed next to him. He could tell he was on the second floor, but that was all he knew.

Eliza moved close to him and began talking. "You killed four or five Roman soldiers, one of whom was a centurion. That carries the penalty of death by crucifixion! What were you thinking?" Before he could answer her, the rabbis added to the conversation.

"Young man, you were both brave and foolish to deny Romans their authority," said one of the rabbis.

Caleb replied without thinking. After all, that was part of his identity. "They had just killed my parents and were capturing people from my village, rabbi! What did you think I would do? Let them take us, too?" He slowly used his arms to push himself off the bed, and he was amazed at how little he hurt. Once he was upright, he apologized for his outburst, and the rabbis graciously forgave him, offering him some water to drink and wash with. Caleb looked at the men and said, "I do not think they will figure out who I am or where I am from, since I described them as 'these people' and not 'my people.'"

The men looked at each other and nodded. "You are probably right. We see that you are quick with your tongue and your weapons, especially considering what was around you. The soldiers who survived will most likely take a different post in a different location, and the dead centurion's body will be carried by the surviving villagers to the coast and dropped into the sea as part of their pagan faith. Your use of non-Hebrew Greek will help you elude them. To us, it appears Yahweh's angels were looking out for you. However, the loss of a centurion will demand retribution. We are glad that your instincts took you to this place."

Caleb looked at Eliza and asked, "Where are we?"

"I went back to Kedron, and the people in the synagogue sent us here," she said.

"You are in the house of healing. You are in the city of Kedron. Your parents have visited us many times in the past." They paused to look at each other, then back at both Eliza and Caleb. "We are sad to learn of their passing. We ask that you stay with us for some days, as you have experienced great trauma, and you must trust us to help you begin the journey of healing. For today, we ask nothing of you but to answer some questions and let us care for you. Can you do that?"

"I am too confused to do anything else," Caleb answered. "We submit to your care."

"How did you acquire such shrewd hunting skills, considering that your parents are some of the most esteemed rabbis in all of Judah?"

"I do not know. I guess I never liked all the ceremonies that my parents made me participate in, and I loved heading out into the wild and hunting. I just wanted to be a normal kid, not the son of royalty."

"Your parents' teachings about the Messiah taught us of a way to live without the rules and rituals of old. They gave us a freedom that we could never dream of. We have seen wondrous events in our lifetime, and we will let you stay here and keep you safe as long as is necessary. However, you have defied the rules of Caesar and his lineage, and that carries the penalty of death for all who help you. We have agreed to lie to any authorities about your presence with us. This is a courtesy we are extending to both of you."

Eliza spoke up since Caleb was not about to answer the question. She was a bit mad, and it showed in her answer.

"His uncle taught him the joys of hunting. And my dad. His uncle, I mean our uncle, was a Roman legate before he retired and joined us," she said.

Caleb nodded his head in agreement.

"Thank you, kind masters. Yeah, that was my uncle Rufus," Caleb said, trying to close this dialog.

"You are welcome."

The rabbis left. Caleb and Eliza sat on the bed for a few minutes before speaking.

Eliza spoke first. "You were delirious after the wound on your head got worse, and I put you on the horse with me. I rode directly here, and these men tended to your wounds. While you were asleep, you kept dreaming out loud, saying, 'We have to get to Titus! We have to see Titus!' What are you talking about? What is your plan?"

"I was dreaming out loud?" he questioned, using a tone of astonishment. He continued. "Huh. Well, my parents are gone, and all I can think about is getting your parents back. The best way to do that is to get both immunity and assistance from Rome. I grabbed Uncle Rufus's ring. I think if we can get an audience with the emperor, I can show him the ring and convince him to write us a royal decree that will free your parents."

"How well did that work for Moses when he went to the Pharaoh, asking him to let our ancestors go?"

"I thought about that. We have a relationship with this new Pharaoh. We know his best friend as our uncle!"

She did not say anything back but only stared at him with an open mouth. She nodded, acknowledging that his idea was pretty good. But what caught her subconscious attention was that his idea was full of adventure. But she wouldn't give him the words of affirmation he was looking for.

"That is all I have, Eliza."

"Well, I was thinking of going home and getting the elders to give us enough gold to buy them out of slavery. We have enough of it, I am sure, but I do not know how much a slave costs, nor do I have a clue where they are now. And if we do find them, what is to say Romans won't just take the gold and make all of us slaves?"

She did not wait for him to answer her.

"I do not think the village elders would get deeply involved in their rescue, though. They always place the village ahead of the individual. They would tell me that this is the way of things. But I do not want to give up on them. I just want my parents back! Why did they follow me to Tamar? They said I could go alone!"

She put her head back on Caleb's chest. He kissed her head and rubbed her hair. She was his only family now. He needed her.

"I do not know what to say. My parents are dead. I saw my dad breathe his last," he said, rubbing her head gingerly. He took a long pause before speaking again.

"Father told me more than once that the Messiah said it is a great joy to die for your faith in Him. He told me that when he died, he wanted it to be because he was teaching that Yeshua resurrected. He asked me to promise not to mourn his death if that happened, and I agreed. I just do not know how to do that, now," said Caleb, wrapping both his huge arms around petite Eliza. She closed her eyes and let him care for her. She, too, was hurting.

"Mother always agreed with him when he said that craziness. She told me that not even death could separate her from Yeshua, and all I can think about now is that she is with Him. Did your parents ever tell you about the teachings of John and the stories he had of what the new kingdom of God is like?"

"Yeah, um, actually, I learned about that from your mom, not mine. My mom did not talk about Yeshua very often. She always told me, 'Ask you auntie!'" With that, both of them erupted in laughter, and Eliza imitated her mother perfectly. Once they stopped laughing, she continued.

"We have got to do something, Cousin. Something is better than nothing. I do not know if I like your plan or if it works, but I'm in. Let's go to Rome and attempt to meet with Titus. Uncle Rufus did talk about him a lot. I feel like I know him enough not to be scared when we meet."

"We are barely of age for bar mitzvah or bah mitzvah, and we are going to try to get an audience with the ruler of the world! That would make our parents proud!"

"Agreed! It's on the other side of the sea, and the last time I checked, we do not have a boat, and neither of us has any experience in this sort of thing."

They both began laughing again at the absurdity of their predicament, allowing some of the healing to start.

"Well, thank you for supporting my ideas. That is what my mom did every time my dad came up with something that had never been done before. It worked for them."

She rolled her eyes. "I am your cousin, not your wife. Frankly, this idea stinks like camel hair after a summer rain."

Caleb could tell she was lying. He jumped on her and held her down, starting to tickle her under her arm. "Well, daughter of Katya and Matthew. What wisdom can you share?"

Eliza tried to get up, but she was laughing too hard. She tried to tell Caleb to stop, but he just kept on tickling her, and she could never finish the words.

His parents were right. She was his family, now. It would be troublesome if she weren't. It still might be troublesome.

For now, though, the rabbis had promised to care for them. They needed time to plan.

"We have been in this room since yesterday evening, talking and mourning the losses we just experienced. And I am hungry!" said Caleb.

"Me, too," Eliza added. "The day is already halfway over."

They both got up, washed their hands and face with the bowl of water and a clean towel that the rabbis had left for them, and went to find the kitchen.

HOUSE OF HEALING

Part 2

Caleb and Eliza remained in what they now called the "house of healing" for another three days. Two other boys from Tamar, who were younger than Caleb, also appeared at the house a day later, and the group participated in some activities that the rabbis had prepared for them to help them share their losses with each other. These younger boys had also lost their parents during the attack, but they had family in the city with who they would now live. Only Eliza and Caleb spent the night in the house. The two other boys stayed with their extended family and would return to their new homes each day before dinner.

All of them had experienced a great loss. Their grief and anger would have been too much had the rabbis not been there to help them. These men had guided many who had lost loved ones at the hands of the Romans, and they knew how to begin the healing process after deaths caused by the atrocities of war and enemy occupation. Indeed, that is why the house of healing existed. Caleb had lost his father and mother. Eliza's parents had been captured and put in chains by Roman soldiers. Eliza's plight was exacerbated in that she had an uncertainty of her parents' whereabouts. She thought they probably were being transported to a Roman slave market, perhaps to be sold, but she did not know. They might already be dead. The rabbis did not make light of the reality that her parents had lost their freedom and that nothing short of a royal decree or a lot of coins could undo that.

The rabbis became their confidantes and teachers. During the first full day after their loss, Dor, the eldest rabbi, had seen them leave the kitchen and walk outside the city walls, and he followed. Once he found them, he began his craft of helping them come to terms with their trauma.

"Greetings, young ones. I wish to talk to you about a different part of your experience in Tamar a few days ago. Are you open to this?"

"Sure, I guess," Caleb said, as he was required to speak as the oldest male in the group.

"You are the son of two murdered parents. Can you tell me what this makes you feel?" he asked.

Caleb paused. This act of thinking before speaking was rare for him. "I do not know…No, I do know! I felt glad that I was able to kill some of them. They can never do that again to anyone else!"

"Your body language is that of someone who is glad, is it?" the rabbi asked in a flat tone.

"No," Caleb admitted. "It isn't. I am not glad. I am still really mad that they're gone. They were serving the Lord! Why does the world kill people who are doing good?"

"Caleb, you have already learned the great lesson that seeking revenge does not remove the pain. Vengeance is the Lord's possession, not ours. I am sure you heard your parents teach this. After all, I learned it from them. Little ones, you have much sorrow and grief, and I share it with you. These people were also my teachers. You have done nothing wrong, but neither have you been abandoned by God. We have prepared a gathering for you this evening, and we want to be with you and pray with you." With that, he led them back into the city.

That evening, many people from the city who attended the local Yeshuaian synagogue came to the house of healing, as word had gotten out that there were the children of two great teachers who had been martyred the day before. The community served a great feast for the four youth. Nearly everyone spoke to Caleb, reminding him that their parents had made a great difference in their lives, and he should be proud of them. Some of them showed him the place where his father and mother used to come and teach. One younger woman talked told Caleb the story of how his parents performed a joint wedding ceremony for her and her husband only a few years ago. Their first-born son was named "Mishi," after his father.

Caleb bent over and extended a single finger to the boy. He took it. "You have a beautiful name, Master Mishi. Did you know that was my father's name?" Caleb had never taught the young children before, but he had seen his mother do so, and he used words that he thought his mother might use. The little boy nodded, a bit afraid and perhaps in awe of the boy in front of him who towered over nearly everyone else in the synagogue.

For the most part, though, Caleb seldom spoke other than to thank the visitors. He kept looking around to make sure he could see the little boy. "A piece of my father lives in him, now," he thought.

Many people also spoke to Eliza about her loss. She told them that her family had been captured and that she would find them. They gave her words of encouragement and a promise to pray that she would find her parents in the days ahead.

After the meal, the slaves cleaned everything, and the group went into the synagogue. The elders sat them down next to the altar, and everyone began to pray and speak to them. The prayers continued for a short time before the lead rabbi stood at the altar and called forward a group of young girls. They were dressed in white clothing with perfectly groomed hair that had been let down, attire normally reserved for special ceremonies or alone time with their husbands. All the girls were virgins, as was required of members of the worship dance team.

One of them stepped forward and spoke to Eliza and Caleb. "Your mother, young Caleb, and your aunt, young Eliza, was our favorite teacher. She convinced us that as women, we can control the outcomes of our families more than anyone else. She was also our hero and our friend. We have created this worship dance, and we wish to perform it for the two of you. Please be patient with us, as we have never performed it. In honor of Yael, we commit to never performing it again until we are with the Messiah." She could not finish telling them of her commitment before she covered her face and wept. Caleb reached over and interlocked his fingers in Eliza, as both were unable to speak due to the power of the moment.

Those in the gathering who had not yet mourned now did so, knowing that they were witnessing a unique event. A young boy carrying a drum made from goat hide and another boy with a flute came from the other side of the altar and played a dirge. The girls separated and began the dance. Their motions were graceful, and they alternated between approaching the altar and gliding away from it. This went on for some time before the girls stepped to surround the altar and locked their hands together. With that, each of the girls sang a short prayer for the martyred teachers and asked for

God's peace to pour itself on all those who felt the loss. As each girl finished their prayer, they knelt before the altar with their hands held high.

Once they had finished, the room was silent, and many in attendance returned to their weeping. After a time, Rabbi Benji came up and thanked everyone for attending and dismissed them. One congregational member asked if they were taking up a collection for the children, but Eliza quickly dismissed the idea, asking for the money to be sent to help rebuild the damage done in Tamar. Each of the girls from the worship group came forward and embraced Eliza, as was a Jewish custom, stepping to the side to allow the next girl to come forward. When the last dancer was done, they all placed a single hand on Eliza and lifted their remaining hands to the sky. The first girl spoke a prayer for Eliza, inviting her to visit them again. Eventually, the rabbis dismissed the crowd, and everyone raised their voices, saying, "So be it." They began leaving the synagogue and walking home with their lamps guiding them.

It was cold and snowing outside the synagogue, as the elements of winter had reached the heart of Judah. Eliza and Caleb were taken to their room, but they felt disoriented from the impact of this evening's event. The exhaustion of the evening's corporate sharing had spent all of their emotional energy, and both of them were ready for bed. The other two children left to go to their new homes. Eliza and Caleb slept all night long and shared their dreams when they woke up.

DEPARTURE FROM THE CITY

By the fourth morning, all the swelling on Caleb's forehead where the centurion's armor had hit was gone, and the stinging in his wrist was gone, thanks to the skills of the herbalist in the house. Caleb already knew how to clean a puncture wound caused by an animal, but he knew nothing of what types of plants and leaves to put on it to speed up healing. The herbalist talked through how she prepared the plants that she used and even showed Caleb how she stored them. She shared all the best places to find them and encouraged Caleb to begin collecting them, as these plants always had a use. Caleb felt as if he were in school again, and it felt good to be learning something new that he could apply to his hunting. He wondered if this healer was also one of his parent's students, but he did not ask. He appreciated the herbalist's willingness to teach him, and they exchanged lots of stories as she cared for the wound on his head no less than twice a day.

Caleb went outside, although he feared being identified by Roman authorities. For safety reasons, the rabbis had Caleb shave his beard to be more anonymous. In addition, he wore the sackcloth clothing of a common man. He would remain outside until late in the afternoon, and Eliza would come and join him. Their routine was to walk outside the city gates and look at the sunset and talk, waiting for the last call of the city crier before returning inside the gates before they closed for the evening. Either Rabbi Dor or Benji would always accompany them, asking them questions and holding them while they cried. It wasn't until the last evening that the tears began to stop, and the insight that comes from passing through grief began to appear.

"I was told by some of the boys in Correae that the setting sun over the sea was beautiful and peaceful," Eliza said on their last evening. "They say it creates a unique feeling of peace."

"Most of the boys in Tamar are too scared to travel to the coast, or if they do, they are within the walls of a city behind the doors of an inn by sunset," Caleb shared.

Eliza told Caleb of Correae's cultural mandate that everyone, not just the boys, travels overnight away from the home so they could learn commerce skills and currency management. She showed Caleb the extra gold coin that she got from her parents. She held the purse of gold and silver at eye level. "You know, we have a lot of money. In fact, we have enough to buy our own wagon, a few camels, perhaps even a slave if we need to. This is pure gold from our village, not the unrefined junk that the Romans use to make coins. But we cannot use our money that way. Our village elders have taught us that big transactions draw big attention, and our village's survival depends on protecting secrecy. We need to be as frugal as we can if we want to travel to Rome without any unnecessary attention. A low profile is the best profile, they say."

"I would prefer to get on a horse and ride there in a day or two. We do not want to waste any time finding your parents."

"And what do you think would happen if a couple of teenagers ran across the plains, leaving a cloud of dust behind them? We would draw the attention of everyone in that part of Judah before we made it halfway. You cannot be that stupid, can you?" Eliza's sarcasm was well-developed for a thirteen-year-old.

"Shut up, cousin." He had forgotten that he might now be a marked man. She was right. They needed to keep a low profile for the time being.

Rabbi Dor had listened to them formulate their plan to travel to Rome and see an audience with the emperor, and he asked them many questions that they had not yet asked themselves. Once he saw Rufus's ring, signifying his office of the legate, he took it to the other rabbis. The rabbis decided that it was too risky to send details of their plan to Correae using a courier, so two of them agreed to personally carry the message to the elders in Correae. They also agreed that no part of the message would be written down. If the Romans ambushed them, they wanted there to be no evidence on them that they were harboring a fugitive.

Eliza, for her part, did not disclose any detail of their village's wealth. However, she was concerned that she might have said too much to Caleb. But she could do nothing about this now, other than to pray and feel guilty. She had become good at both of these activities lately. Like her aunt, she hated keeping secrets.

The rabbis added what assistance they could to their plan as it formed. There were specific docks at the port that were more friendly to Jews than others, and they gave them names to ask for at one of the synagogues outside of town that they could use as their base while they awaited a passage over the sea. Normally, trips to Rome took months to plan, finance, and accommodate, as precautions had to be taken to guard resources while away. Care of livestock and fields of grain had to be addressed, as well as protection of the home and other personal property, such as carts and raw iron reserves. It was decided that two rabbis would return to Tamar, letting the leadership know that Caleb had survived and was going to Rome to seek a decree from the emperor to free his aunt and uncle. From there, the rabbis would continue their journey on horseback to Correae to let the elders know what had happened to Katya, Matthew, and their daughter Eliza. Once there, they would return to the city and continue to pray for the two of them until they returned. They asked that Caleb and Eliza return to the house of healing once they came back from Rome, as they had other things to share with them that could only be shared then. Although they did not know what that meant, they agreed.

Rabbi Benji gave them final guidance on the evening of the fourth day. "There are groups leaving the city gates every morning, and at least one of them is heading to the coast. Tomorrow, there is a couple with four wagons that is also going directly to Joppa. They will let you go with them at no cost, as a favor to our mission, so you can save your village's money, Eliza. You must appear to be workers if any Romans enter their encampments at the end of the days. You must discard your Hebrew clothing and buy new cloth when you reach Rome."

"I take it all off when I go hunting, anyway," said Caleb. The rabbi chuckled.

"I should have known," he said, putting his hand on the boy's shoulder.

"That sounds pretty easy," Eliza added. "How long will it take to get to Joppa?"

"It is two nights on the plains from here, and you arrive near mid-day on the third day."

"Benji, do you know the people who are in this caravan?" asked Eliza. The rabbi had long ago given them permission to call him only by his first name.

"I know of them, but I had never spoken to them before yesterday. I think you can trust them with some of your story, but do not tell them all of it. They are friendly but not proven yet to be friends. I am assuming you know the difference." Eliza closed her eyes and nodded in affirmation.

Once a month, Eliza's family cooked and served all fifty families in Correae, and she knew how to plan and execute mass food services. For her, it was common sense to know what sort of preparations were required for them to go on an extended trip such as this one. She remembered how her mother had stood next to her as she made ready all the provisions that she and her father would need the first time that they traveled to the Jerusalem area three years ago. Eliza purchased several loaves of fresh bread, and she wrapped them in a clean, wet cloth to keep them fresh. She purchased dried fruits and meats in case it was not possible to start a cooking fire the next two nights. She carried extra rope, cloth, metal nails, and a sharp knife. She purchased two bedrolls made from a blend of camel and Egyptian cotton. She had a piece of leather and three skins for water, knowing from experience that they needed two water storage systems and a backup. She had a change of clothes that she wrapped in sheepskin treated with a light amount of mustard oil, keeping the contents waterproof. In the waterproof sheepskins, she also kept a small but thicker wool cloak, a flint, a small piece of steel, and some kindling to start a fire. She added a warm, wool cap, as she had heard that Rome was colder than Judah, and she wanted to be comfortable during the winter days as they sailed north into the Roman harbor. She had some wool socks and wool mittens, as well.

Eliza also knew from experience that carrying items to trade with in distant lands helps establish credibility and gives one a chance to interact with the culture. She knew that everything in the world was available for purchase on the streets of Rome. She asked around in the market and found that purple dyes and Jewish cinnamon fetched high prices on the streets of Rome. Eliza filled both of their backpacks with cinnamon, hoping to sell it once they arrived. She purchased only as much as was reasonable in the marketplace, so any interested merchant might see that they were covering their costs and making some profit, but not enough profit to justify additional scrutiny. Most of Eliza's wealth remained in gold and silver coin, unseen to the outside world.

She divided the coins into four different stashes. She and Caleb each carried the equivalent of half a year's wage on their person, and they kept another two year's wages in the bottom of their backpacks. No one judging them from the outside would ever conclude that they were carrying such immense wealth. Eliza still carried the allotment of gold meant for the synagogue school. It had been burned down, now, but she kept the coins, not really sure what she would do with them.

While Eliza was taking care of their financial situation and traveling rations, Caleb was restocking his weapon supply. He took his knives to a local blacksmith and had them sharpened, and he took some of Eliza's money to buy a small steel sword that he could hide in his backpack. He did not tell Eliza how much he spent, as he found her stinginess with money annoying. He also replaced his arrows and got two replacement bowstrings.

The following morning, they met Peter and Elisha, the caravan leader and his wife. Eliza offered to pay them to take them to the coast, but they refused, telling them to climb in one of four carts of olive oil they were taking to Joppa. They were friendly and offered each of them an orange before leaving. Oranges were readily available in Judah this time of year, and they tasted wonderful.

The trip was uneventful by every measure. Along the three-day journey, the couple stopped for the night in known small towns, and Eliza and Caleb adopted a policy of speak-only-when-spoken-to. No one ever asked their names or where they were from. Peter introduced them as cousins from inland Judah who had a personal matter to attend to in Joppa. No one seemed to care. Caleb and Eliza slept well, ate plenty of food, and seldom talked during the day about their plans to go back home. The rest and lack of heavy exertion caused Caleb's wounds to heal nearly completely, and Eliza was grateful for that.

On the third day, when they reached the outskirts of Joppa in the middle of the morning, they finally asked Peter and Elisha a question.

"We need to find a passage to Rome," Eliza said. "What do you recommend?"

The couple looked at each other and smiled. "This time of year, that request is easy to accommodate. Once we reach the port and unload our olive oil, I can ask our buyer if he has a need for anyone on the ship taking it to Rome. People are traveling between this part of the Empire and Rome every day. It should not be hard to find a passage."

Caleb jumped in. "We do not want to work on the boat or get a free passage. Neither of us has even been on the sea, and we are a little scared. We want a safe passage with a room below deck, and we will gladly pay for it."

Eliza agreed with him for what seemed like the first time in a while.

"We will ask for you about that," Peter said.

Shortly thereafter, they arrived at the docks. They climbed out of the wagon and gazed on one of the most magical things they had ever laid their eyes upon. Never before had they seen a body of water as big as the Mediterranean. Unlike the Sea of Galilee, there was no other side to see. It was as if sailing west would mean falling off the end of the world. The port was bustling with activity, and there were many people on wooden docks that led from the land into the sea to allow the loading and unloading of seagoing vessels. Caleb and Eliza watched as no fewer than twenty boats spread across six docks were in some stage of loading or unloading. The older couple let them sit there while they walked up and down the docks, asking some questions to find a boat for Caleb and Eliza to board that was going to Rome.

Part of the training that the rabbis had taught them was to find gratitude in all things, especially when they felt the loss of their parents. After gazing at all the activity for a while, Caleb grabbed Eliza's hand, and they both got down on their knees. Caleb prayed first. "Messiah, thank You for bringing us here uneventfully. Thank You for giving us Your servants in the city to help us begin our healing. We ask that the mercy You showed us to bring us safely here is something we can extend to others as we continue on our journey. Thank You for my cousin and her help to get us here. Let us find her parents."

Eliza kept her eyes closed. "Yeshua, what he said goes for me as well. Give us a safe passage to Rome and let our pathway to Titus be one that brings You all the glory!"

"Amen," they both said.

"I see you are going to try to see the emperor," said Peter, as he had heard their prayers. He had approached them while they were still praying, but they were not aware of his presence until he spoke.

They looked at each other before Caleb spoke up. "We do. Have you been to his palace in the Palatine Hill? I hear it is beautiful."

The trader of olive oil laughed. "I do not think any Jew has ever been there unless they were a slave!"

"We ask, kind sir, that you not tell anyone what you heard us pray," Eliza said.

"Well, if you are going to pray out loud, you must know there shall always be consequences to displaying our faith in public." With that remark, Caleb and Eliza realized that Peter and his wife were also Yeshuaians.

"That sounds like something that my parents would say," Caleb said.

"We must not be afraid of displaying our faith publicly. Thank you for reminding us!"

Peter smiled then turned towards some approaching dock hands who would often help him unload his oil.

"Try the third dock from the end," he said.

Caleb and Eliza thanked him. They grabbed their backpacks and walked towards what they hoped would be their ride to Rome.

SETTING SAIL

Due to the direction of the wind, the vessel that Caleb and Eliza booked their passage on, a medium-sized boat, was scheduled to depart at noon tomorrow. The greatest risk of wreck occurred near shores, and the direction of the wind travel away from the coast of Judah was westerly this time of year but only predictable at mid-day.

Once they learned that they would be on the boat for up to two weeks, they immediately made a trip back to the markets of Joppa. "We have got to get more provisions before we leave in case something happens. We need to buy an extra barrel of drinking water as well as some more fruit. Remember how they taught us about that sea disease where you do not get enough fruit?" Eliza talked quickly, meaning she was either excited or scared. Caleb wondered who she was really talking to. It definitely wasn't him. She gave him no time to answer her questions.

Caleb smiled, as he knew better than to react to all of her concerns. There would be twenty other people on the boat besides them, including crew, and there would be food, even if they had to ration it. "I am more concerned about the unexpected than I am about delays caused by weather. I think we should buy two sheep bladders that have been treated in olive oil, so if we capsize, we can float."

They decided they would do the shopping together. That meant Eliza would be in charge. Much of that afternoon, the local shopkeepers that they spoke with gave them advice about how to travel by sea. One man had come from Rome several years earlier, and he assured them that boats made the journey up to twice a month.

One older man shared a piece of valuable advice. "Just because you have no experience and are scared doesn't mean that everyone else is. There will be many people working on the boat who know what they are doing, even if you do not." That gave both of them some assurance.

The next day, they boarded the ship staring at the twin-sailed vessel in wonder. Neither had been on a boat that had a below-deck section, and they quickly walked through it, looking at all the rooms and storage features, realizing that this was more like a small inn than a boat. Soon, the winds took them away from land at a pace much faster than they had ever experienced. Caleb and Eliza stood at the front of the boat, closed their eyes, and felt the salty air strike their faces as they proceeded due west. The combination of cooler air temperatures and the motion of the sea created none of the ill side effects that either of them had been warned about. They stared at the horizon in the distance and did not focus on the motion of the boat.

The two sails that propelled the boat were made of great rolls of white cloth. The ropes that held them up were thin, made of unique materials from the Far East. These ropes were smooth and light, stronger than the thickest of ropes used in Judah to carry timber and stone. As Caleb and Eliza admired them, the captain called down to the front of the boat in Greek. "Never seen silk before, have you?" he asked.

"No, we haven't," Eliza replied. "It is amazing. Where did you get it?"

"I bought all of it at a market in Rome with the coin I got from carrying soldiers."

Caleb looked up at him, holding the end of the rope. "Does it burn like hemp rope does?"

"It does. Smells like burned feathers. It shrinks first, though. Just add some vinegar after it burns, and it cleans up nicely. You two citizens heading home?"

They had never been told that they looked like Roman citizens before now. "We are not," responded Eliza. The tone in the conversation went limp as the question begged for more than a yes or no answer.

"Then what are you going to Rome for?" the captain asked. He had no fear of their answer. He was their driver, and he was going to talk to them over these next two weeks. They might as well get used to answering his questions.

Caleb decided a partial answer would work. "We need to get a document from there and bring it back to handle a transaction we are working on. It involves some other people too. We are hoping for an uneventful ride, as neither of us has been on the sea before." Caleb was counting on his father's teachings on how to guide a conversation. Mishi had demonstrated that to make the shift, he needed to end the first conversation with a new one that the listener would think he was an expert in. Caleb's question practically begged the captain to tell stories of their adventures, and the idea worked perfectly. For the rest of the afternoon, Caleb and Eliza listened to the captain and his two crew members tell tales of their travels at sea. Both of the young Hebrews laughed as often as the conversation allowed, and both gave compliments to the men at each chance, just as they had been taught. There was nothing more valuable for them to establish on this first day at sea than a relationship with the crew who would keep them well-fed and safe.

As the sun neared late afternoon, the captain told the two other crew to go down and prepare the evening meal. He planned to retire to his quarters for an afternoon nap like most crew and passengers.

"I'm going down too," Caleb said in quiet Hebrew. "Those guys talked my ear off,"

Eliza stayed at the front of the boat. After a few minutes, she found herself deep in prayer, asking Yahweh to help them secure an audience with everyone they needed to along the way. She spoke in Hebrew under her breath, and she kept her eyes closed.

She was startled by a voice in her ear. "Hey, little girl, what are you doing all alone on this here boat?"

She knew enough from her travels to and from Tamar that the members of the ship's crew who she now saw before her had been drinking alcohol, like the ones in the taverns she saw the first time she visited Hebron with her father. She turned, feeling a fear not unlike the fear she had felt seeing Tamar in flames.

Before she could act, the man closest to her took another step forward. "I think you shall be our entertainment on this boat," he said, smiling at her, displaying a mouth only partially full of teeth. He was a disgusting site to Eliza.

One of the men moved to her right, and one stood in front of her. The men on each side grabbed her upper arms and held her against the ropes on the edge of the front of the boat, while the man in front of her began to untie the string that held up his pants. "You might be the best part of this little boat ride, little girl!" he said with a smile that further put his bad dental work on display.

Eliza remembered some of what she had talked about with her aunt, and she screamed. Her aunt had done nothing when the Roman soldier raped her, and but Eliza was not going to be raped without a fight. "Let go of me! Let go of me, you animals!" she screamed, nearly in hysterical rage. However, due to the roar of the seas and the wind, her words quickly died out in the air.

"Oh, this is how I like them!" said the man in front of her as he finished untying the last of his strings.

"Help!" she yelled.

The man in front stuffed a piece of cloth down her throat and covered her mouth with a neckerchief that muted her efforts to make noise. She tried to scream, but it was muffled.

"Hold her down, boys. You will each get your turn. We are going to be on this boat many more days." They began pulling her to the deck of the ship. The man in front bent down to take off her lower garments.

The man suddenly stopped and grunted, lurching forward slightly. A wink of an eye later, he then made another lurching motion, but not towards her. Instead, he twisted himself halfway around and attempted to stand up. There was a pair of arrows sticking out of his backside, one in the upper leg, the other in his buttocks. The man blocked Eliza's view, but as he turned, she saw a familiar sight. It was her cousin's forearm, wrapping around the man's neck.

Caleb must have heard her scream. Caleb dragged the man to the deck with him, never relenting his hold on the man's throat. Everyone could see that the man was fighting but was also no longer breathing. Both of the arrows had broken off at the skin, with the metal tip and wooden shaft now deeply in the man's body. The more he fought, the deeper the tips of the arrows traveled into his meat.

Caleb addressed the two remaining men. "This man will die in the next few seconds. Swear on your family's honor that you will leave my cousin alone, or you will meet the same fate as this scoundrel."

Before the men could respond, Caleb pushed the injured man over the edge of the boat. Jumping to his feet, Caleb moved to the place where Eliza was now on the ground. He looked both of the men in the eyes as they knelt next to Eliza. "I did not say that I would kill him. I will let the sharks do that for me. He will bleed out from his backside in the sea, and he will receive the death he deserves."

Caleb reached down and drew his hunting knife from his boot. He held it equidistant from the men's faces, as they had not yet released their hold on Eliza.

"Who's next?" he asked, switching eye contact between the two men.

Both men attempted to move away from the edge of the boat. They were not prepared for such cunning resistance and were scared for their lives. They released their hold on Eliza, and she jumped to place Caleb between the men and herself.

Caleb spoke to her in a slang version of Hebrew that he hoped only she would understand. "Go to the hold and get out my sword. Bring it to me while I talk to these guys."

She got up and walked as quickly as she could to the sleeping holds below deck while Caleb pushed one of the men into the other. "So, this is what a good time looks like for you? Guess what? Today is your lucky day. I am the offspring of a rape, and I swore an oath to kill any man I ever saw raping a woman. Who will be fed to the sharks next? You did not answer my question yet. I need to show you something first."

Before the men could speak, he reached into his pocket and pulled out Rufus's ring. He put it on and showed it to them. "Unless, of course, you are greater than the nephew of a Roman legate who just witnessed a crime committed by three cowards," he said. In the moment, he was tempted to cower over them, smiling and increasing his threatening words. However, the words of Uncle Rufus came back to his mind.

"Use power to the extent that you must, not the extent that you want to. An abuse of power will haunt your soul when you cross that line," he would tell his young nephew.

These men could now see that they were in over their heads.

"Or would you prefer crucifixion?" were the words he wanted to speak. Instead, he chose not to speak, awaiting Eliza's imminent return.

Caleb had the element of surprise moments earlier, but now it was one man against two, and despite his size, any orchestrated attack by the two of them could mean his downfall. Caleb had been speaking loudly enough that the captain could hear him, counting on him coming to investigate what all the calamities were.

Caleb glanced down and saw that both men were wearing leather leggings and foot coverings, and he created a plan to assert himself and take away their advantage.

When the next wave hit the boat, he yelled out, "Look at that!" as he lowered his knife. As they turned, he pushed both of the men, sending one over the railing and into the sea. The other one fell over the side of the boat but grabbed the rope railing. He hung over the edge of the boat, holding on with one hand.

Eliza came back, running towards Caleb. "Your sword! When did you get this?" she said, handing it to him.

Caleb took the sword and pointed it at the man. "You have two choices now. Let go and swim or give me your hand and lose your entrails."

The man looked at the sword and spoke. "I am sorry. Please! I am sorry."

Eliza spoke to Caleb rapidly in Hebrew. "This man may deserve death but remember the lessons on forgiveness that your parents taught us. We all deserve to die for our actions. We are not the judge, even though we live in a world where all men want to judge. Let him live, Caleb."

She leaned over the railing and extended her hand to the man without looking at him. She spoke in common Greek that all would understand.

"Give me your arm. My cousin will not kill you."

Caleb put the sword in his belt and also reached down to help the man up. They pulled him back onto the deck, where he lay in a state of shock.

The captain was now next to them. He needed no explanation as to what had happened. He kicked the man in the ribs. "Get up, you camel! You owe your life to the young girl you tried to rape, for I can tell you, the boy would have done exactly what he said if it wasn't for her stepping in. Go down into the galley and stay there! I will let this son of a legate decide what to do with you once we reach Roman land again."

The man fled to the galley below. As he left, the captain looked at Caleb. "Speaking Hebrew and carrying a legate's ring. Boy, there has got to be a story there!" As the man stepped below the line of sight into the galley, the captain grumbled. "Seems like something like this happens all the time nowadays. And you two owe me a story!" he said, pointing at both of them.

Caleb finally turned to Eliza and let her hug him. Even though only a few moments had passed, it seemed like an entire day. All the while, the captain stood next to both of them, realizing that he might have some liability for letting what appeared to be a Roman citizen get assaulted.

"If he comes up again, you can kill him," the captain offered. "At sea, there is no law other than what the captain says. I say that he is a coward and a rapist, and you can do whatever you want to him. Based on who that ring says you are, he is dead, anyway."

Caleb thanked the captain, and he took Eliza down into the hold and into their room. He let her tell her story, and he held her close to him the rest of the day.

Caleb reacted as a man would and should react; that is what he told himself. He was protecting his family, just as his father had told him to protect Eliza. However, he now found that he had killed men in consecutive weeks, and his soul was feeling the effects. He continually recalled the look on their faces as he pushed them over the edge of the boat and into the sea. The horror on their faces had burned a scar onto his soul, and he knew it would haunt him. Just as Dor and Benji had told him: killing always appears to be a part of fixing something; it also creates new wounds.

He never intended to take a life, but he did. He would have taken more, except that his reason to take the life told him not to kill anymore. Eliza was a better person than he was. She acted like she really needed him since she was nearly a victim of rape. What he was not about to tell her was that he needed her at least as much. It would have been easy for him to kill the last man and not lose sleep. After all, that man deserved it.

That evening, Caleb got up to relieve himself over the edge of the boat. The captain was doing the same thing.

"That is a strong-willed cousin you got there. How in the hell did she get the courage to tell you to leave that man alone? I tell you, I would have done exactly what you said you were going to do and not thought twice about it."

Caleb did not answer but only nodded his head in agreement, staring at the moonlight reflecting off the sea waves.

"She has that kind of heart, huh?" said the captain.

"Like her aunt and uncle," said Caleb. Caleb flashed back to the scene in Tamar just over a week ago when he killed trying to protect his family. He relived it, just like the rabbis said he would.

"Captain, one week ago, I killed four or five people trying to protect her mother and father and my mother and father. Right now, I feel just like it did the day after I killed them. Why is it the thing that I do not wish to do is the very thing that I do?" he asked.

"That is a great question that has been asked through the ages. When I was younger, I would drink too much wine, swearing never to do that again. You know what would happen? I would do it again a few days later, wondering what happened. Seems to me that your wine takes the form of a bow and a sword."

Caleb looked at him when he made his analogy. It resonated to Caleb's core, and it hurt. He knew what a drunk was; he did not want to be one.

"So, what am I supposed to do?" he asked.

"Do what your cousin there did. Figure out how to forgive. Spend time with people who know how to withhold their desire to unsheathe a blade. Avoid the Roman military. I am telling you this with certainty. They will try to recruit you and get you to join their ranks if they haven't already done so. Shooting a bow accurately on the deck of a boat is no easy task. Just make sure you politely say, 'no,' or this haunting you have right now will become a permanent part of your life," he said.

Caleb nodded. Where was this guy last week? As the sun began to set and the sky turned rich red, Caleb broke the silence between the two of them.

"Who do you pray to?" Caleb asked.

"I do not know. I am still working on that," said the captain.

"Do you know about the Messiah?" Caleb asked.

"Messiah?" the captain said.

"Yeah, let me tell you His story," he said. Caleb stood next to the man as he unwound the mystery of Yeshua on the cross, answering the man's questions. The matter-of-fact nature of both men made the conversation relatively fast, with a lot of head-nodding as each processed what the other said.

All the while, Eliza stood at the top of the stairs leading down into the galley, with her hands lifted high into the sky, praying for her cousin and the captain. She knew that Caleb had some great role models as parents who he had surely watched share this message. He needed no guide. He needed protection from the enemy's attempts to foil the outcome that the truth provides.

In that moment, there was no rape. There was no villain. There was no evil other than what exists in the spiritual world. Her aunt had drilled into her that the only enemy that really exists is the one in the spiritual world, and the best weapon a young Hebrew girl can ever unleash is prayer. And she did.

She felt anger depart her soul, and she began to heal, just as the rabbis promised her would happen when she would confront the enemy without shame.

And none of them saw the only surviving attacker from earlier watching all of this.

THE TRUST OF
THE CAPTAIN

There had not been any provocative events since the attempted rape, but Eliza remained cautious and shaken. Her fear of the unknown remained, and she went nowhere without Caleb or the captain within sight, including the bathroom. Caleb insisted that she be near him all the time, and she submitted to his request without resentment.

The captain asked questions of Caleb nearly every day regarding history that he did not know. Caleb remembered much of it, but not all, and he would often ask Eliza to come and complete the holes in his knowledge of the life of Yeshua. She had a better memory for that sort of thing.

They spotted land on the fourth day. They were still too far away to make out any features, but it was great for their soul to see land again. Everyone came to the bow of the boat to see the outcropping of rocks and land in the distance. Eliza went to the top deck with the captain and deckhands, as she was always invited to spend time in the "crew only" section of the boat. She was accustomed to being there, as she thought it to be the safest place in the boat. The captain was used to her answering his tougher questions regarding the mysteries of the trinity of God and forgiveness of sins, and he had grown fond of her over the last few days. For her part, Eliza was glad to answer them.

Their dialog switched between her greenhorn knowledge of sailing and the Roman Empire and his beginner status as a Yeshuaian. They found each other equally valuable. With land on the horizon, Eliza had many more questions than the captain.

"Is that Rome?" she asked.

"No, dear, that isn't the city of Rome, but the land on both sides of it is owned by Rome. The land to the left is a large island called Sicily. The land to the right is Calabria, and there is a port called Messene on Sicily that we will stop at. Once we get there, we will get some provisions and be on our way the following day. After that, we will be about three days of sailing from the river ports in Rome."

Eliza looked worried. Sailing was not in her arsenal of activities that brought her peace.

"How much colder will it get as we head north?" she asked.

"Not much more than now. Rome feels about the same as the coast of Judah, you know?" he told her rhetorically.

"I am scared, captain. I have never sailed, and this constant motion is something foreign to me," she said.

"We are here for you, young girl," he said reassuringly. "You will be safe with us." Eliza held on to the captain's arm, as she had taken to doing since the attempted rape. He put his free arm around her shoulder and drew her in for a sideways hug. As a Hebrew, this would have been a most inappropriate act, but Eliza knew that these men were not Hebrews, and she had no reason to hold them to standards that they hadn't agreed to. Caleb had seen this and talked with her about the differences in boundaries between Jews and gentiles. They both agreed that there was no need to reprimand them or try to teach them the Hebrew way of interacting with others of the opposite sex who were not family. Truth be told, Eliza really needed the affection of a father figure now.

"It's Eliza," she said. "My name is Eliza, remember?"

"Yeah, I remember. We are here for you, Ms. Eliza," he said, repositioning his arm around her as a father might do. His affection felt good, as she knew he was not like the rapists who had held the same arm that he was holding. It was the same way her father would hold her when he would tell her stories in the evenings. Eliza knew what the healers would say once she and Caleb returned to Judah and then the healing house. The captain was a good guy in a bad situation; he was not part of the bad situation and shouldn't be equated with it.

"Thank you, captain," she said. He only nodded, choosing not to respond with words, but she felt his communication. She felt that he was addressing something deeper, perhaps created when he learned of Yeshua yesterday.

"It is going to be okay, dear," he said.

A STORM THAT DEFINES YOU

The next morning, the captain brought everyone to the top deck at sunrise. He was not an orator like Mishi, but he knew how to get his point across.

"Do you see those red skies? We are in for some bad weather. I am going to try to get us to land before that happens. We will be going as fast as this boat can go. Our goal is to reach Messene on the island of Sicily before the bad weather hits. Be alert because it will get bumpy!" Before everyone started grumbling, he added, "Do not panic. We will be with the sight of land all day long. We will ride along the north shore because it is safer until we reach the village of Calabria. We will then turn hard left and go into the wind until we are near Messene. We will spend time in the harbor until the weather clears. May whoever you pray to protect us as we travel."

The captain still had a way to go with his understanding of what Yeshua can and cannot do.

Caleb looked around at the other passengers on the ship, all conversing with fervor at the news. He had never noticed their identities before now. There was a group of six Roman women who were heading back home after visiting their husbands, and they each had one slave with them. They were by far the loudest group and accounted for half of the boat's allotment of passengers. They all had questions, and they each offered their slave to help the captain and the deckhands with anything they needed. Two older soldiers were traveling home, and no one could tell where they were from, as they spoke a language no one understood. The deckhands thought it was Gaelic, others thought it was Saxon. Either way, no one was courageous enough to ask. They added to the conversation in broken Greek, "Good idea now to drink more!" They raised their fists to the sky and shook them as if this announcement was more about a reason to drink than potential danger. Both of them scared Eliza.

"I'm scared. What are we going to do?" she said, speaking loudly in Hebrew, convinced now that no one could understand her.

Caleb knew what to do with Eliza. Normally, he would suggest that she toughen up. However, she had reason to be emotionally unstable right now, and he empathized with her. She needed something to do to get her singleness of focus on something else. "Let's make sure that the sheep bladders are fully inflated and our goods secured. Would you go below deck and do that?" he asked.

As the skies darkened and the wind and chop picked up, they distracted themselves by staring at Mount Etna on the south side of the Strait of Messene. It was a huge outcropping of a mountain on the island of Sicily. The size of the snow-covered side and the height of the summits had no parallel in Judah nor Egypt, and they were in awe at its immenseness. Each time a wave would come over the sides of the boat, the mountain's greatness got lost, and they were brought back to the reality of their peril. Caleb kept Eliza grounded by reminding her to keep looking at the mountain when the waves hit.

One of the deckhands saw them staring at it. "That is a volcano. It spews hot lava, although that hasn't happened in a long time."

"How long ago is a long time?" asked Eliza, feeling more dread than ever.

"Not since I was born. They say the deadly sea monster Typhon was trapped under that mountain by Zeus himself. The hot rock comes from the forges of Hephaestus underneath all that snow."

Neither of the children had been educated in either Greek or Roman theology, and they had no idea how to respond. They knew of Yeshua and His power, but not of any multi-theistic cults with gods named Typhon and Zeus. But they couldn't deny that smoke was coming from the top of the volcano at the same time that snow was falling on its flanks. They did not understand. Why had they never heard of this place? Had not traveling outside the confines of Judah limited their education this much?

Then, with no warning, they rounded a small point on the northern shore, and large waves began to explode on the sides of the boat. With every swell, water would come over the top deck and onto the boat. With the sun already heading towards the horizon, the mates yelled out to the captain.

"Captain, do we make the turn and head to Messene or keep going through this mess?"

The captain made one last look at the horizon before turning towards the mates and barking his orders.

"If we do not go now, we might have to wait till morning. Switch the sails around. Let's tack south! Do it!"

With that, the two men decreased the pull on one of the sails and increased the pull on the other. The boat turned south and began to speed up rapidly. The force of the wind took them away from shore and directly towards Messene. The bow raised and fell with the swell, but the water no longer came over the edges. Both the crew and passengers held on to anything they could find that was stationary. The pattern appeared to stable, then a large boom came from the front of the boat. The boat stopped moving forward, and two of the women and one of their slaves flew over the edge of the boat and into the sea. The boat had hit something.

The captain called to the crew, demanding some action. "We hit some rocks, and we are taking on water! Move everyone to the back of the boat and see if we can break free!"

The oldest crewman yelled out, "Captain, what's the point of breaking free of the rocks? We are still going to keep taking on water."

"Maybe so, but the boat will at least drift away, and maybe we can save it later. We aren't far from land. No one lives if we stay here. Move!"

Eliza was at the bottom of the stairs and had already inflated the sheep bladders and packed up all their gear into their backpacks. Although she did not see any damage, she heard the wood planks at the front of the boat crack like firewood when they hit. Caleb saw it, standing at the top of the stairs looking down at her when it happened, and he yelled to her.

"Eliza, give me your hand," and she complied. He pulled her to the top deck, then reached down and pulled everything up as quickly as he could. He handed one of the inflated bladders to Eliza, slipped the backpack on her, and loosened its belt around her waist. As he suspected, she was paralyzed. He grabbed both of her forearms and looked her in the eyes. "Cousin, we are getting off this boat! Hold this bladder in front of you and swim to shore. Do not stop until you can stand up and walk to land. I will be there waiting for you. I promise. Watch and follow me." He nodded to her, then jumped off the deck of the boat feet first and disappeared under the waves. He came up from under the water's surface, yelling out her name one more time before he started paddling towards the shore. One of the slaves who was already in the water started to pursue him, but the first swell sent him under the surface, and Eliza never saw him again.

Eliza felt more alone than she ever had in her life. Watching her parents be captured and feeling powerless to do anything had made her feel feeble and weak. Being nearly raped by three men made her feel frail and vulnerable. However, she was now on a sinking boat, and her cousin was already on his way to the shore. Her chest felt hollow, feeling as if it contained some sort of power to prevent her from moving. But she could not die like this. Her aunt would be disappointed. The elders in her village told her to fight and try to escape. Caleb told her exactly how to follow him, and he demonstrated it for her.

Eliza no longer wanted adventure. Were life-threatening risks, like sailing across the ocean in winter, part of an adventure? If that is true, then she did not really want it anymore. She thought she liked the unknown; now, the unknown was preventing her from moving.

"I love you, Little One," was all she heard. It was a man's voice. It was not Caleb's, nor was it her father's. She had never heard it before. He was near her, but Eliza couldn't tell which direction he was from her. Then, she moved.

"You can do this," was the last thing she heard before she felt her feet strike the water's surface, and she submerged. Before Caleb jumped, he told her to keep her eyes closed when she hit the water. When she surfaced, she reopened them when the shock from the water became apparent. She felt the cold winter sea trying to hold her down, but she had the bladder and knew what to do.

She saw that she wasn't the only one in the water. The situation behind her was chaos. She heard more sounds of wood splintering off the bow as the boat tried to separate from the rocks, and she heard screaming and another splash not far from where she landed.

No one was going to take her bladder without a fight. She put it in front of her and began kicking with her legs and traveling towards the north shore. She could see the land, and it was not far away. She kicked very hard, but not so hard that she would run out of strength before she reached the land. She needed to separate from anyone else now in the water who might be coming at her to take her flotation device. She dared not stop and look back. She needed to separate herself from people trying to come after her, just like Caleb did.

She moved, assuming that a threat was in the water, trying to chase her down. What she did not know was that nearly everyone else in the water was clinging to the sides of the boat, even though it was sinking. When she was about halfway to shore, she reached into her soul and extracted enough courage to pause her swim and look back. There were a few other people still holding onto the boat, but now nearly half of it was underwater. She saw motion on the deck as a few of the passengers had not yet abandoned the ship. She also noticed that there were two other people swimming in the same direction she was going. She couldn't identify them, but they were much behind her. She turned back towards Caleb and the land and resumed her kick.

"Be at peace," said the voice. It was still next to her.

"Okay," she answered, and she stopped swimming and took a few breaths to gather herself. "Thank you," was all she could say before the urgency of reaching the land overtook her, and she returned to kicking. Caleb told her that hypothermia would kill her if she stopped, and she was not about to stop fighting.

She had no idea how much time had elapsed since she hit the cold water. She kept moving steadily, but the cold water was draining her energy, and she knew she couldn't stay in the water much longer. The sun was overhead now, but she began to tire. She saw that the person in front of her had reached land and was standing up, waving, and yelling at her. She tried to speak, but her jaw was shaking uncontrollably, and she couldn't form any words, no matter which language she tried. Moments later, she could understand Caleb's voice.

"Keep kicking! Keep kicking! You are almost here! I am coming out to help you. Just key on my voice, Cousin!" She couldn't see him. In fact, everything that she could see was in black and white. She knew the loss of color vision meant her body was shutting down non-essential systems, and color vision was one of them. She had to keep moving. If she did not, she would die.

Suddenly, she felt a force on her forearm, and Caleb was in front of her. He smiled. "This is some cold water, isn't it? Follow me. You're almost there."

"Stand up! I will help you walk in," he said, with his most enthusiastic voice. As soon as she put her feet down and was able to walk, her color vision returned. Concurrently, all fear departed, and she felt the encouragement of her family. Now that she could see the bottom of the sea, she was amazed at how rocky it was and how full of seaweed and small fish.

"Let's get you out of the water and onto dry land. You need to go into the woods and change out of wet clothes as soon as you can," Caleb instructed.

Eliza stepped onto dry land and returned to her paralyzed state. She shivered and nodded in agreement. There were woods adjacent to the shore. The soil was rich in nutrients, with plants growing everywhere. Caleb took off her backpack, and it felt good to lose the weight of that. A moment later, he handed her the dry bag that contained her spare clothes. Caleb pointed towards the woods, saying, "Go! The faster you change, the faster you will get warm!"

She took the first steps towards the woods and realized she would have never made the swim wearing that pack without the bladder. The ground under her feet felt nothing like it did in Judah, as this was soft to the touch and void of rocks. Instead of hot dirt, the ground was covered in moss and lichens. The woods smelled rich with evergreens like pine and spearmint, a lot like Correae did in the fall. The sun felt hotter now that she was out of the water. Caleb kept talking to her as she moved into the woods and out of sight.

"Change fast; do not think, just do it. I will get a fire for you," he said. Caleb was still wearing wet clothes, but he seemed to be less impacted by the cold water than she was.

She came back out from the trees in her dry clothing, feeling numb all over, and sat next to the fire that Caleb had started. Its warmth gave her permission to sit and be idle, allowing her body time to warm up. Caleb handed Eliza some dried meat and a peeled orange. He also had placed a full skin of water next to her, knowing that she would feel her dehydration as soon as she started warming up.

Eliza had only been sitting still for a few minutes when two surviving swimmers made it to land. The first one to reach land was one of the deckhands. He came up out of the water on his own and stood next to the fire. Caleb had been stoking the fire with lots of driftwood, and it was now roaring. The deckhand took off wet outer garments, and Caleb took them to hang over a small shrub to dry, next to Eliza's clothes. He shook uncontrollably, but the heat also warmed him quickly. He was anything but idle, though, and he constantly looked back towards the ship, waving his hands for others to see him.

As the last swimmer neared the shore, the deckhand spoke to Eliza. It was the first words anyone other than Caleb had spoken.

"That is the man who lived after trying to take your body from you," he said, pointing at the last survivor.

"Really?" said Caleb as he grabbed his bow. He notched an arrow and walked towards the shore. "That dirty dog! Who does he think he is, trying to come this way?" He readied himself to shoot an arrow into the man as he stood upon the offshore rocks.

Eliza also stood up and pursued Caleb. She walked up behind him and removed the arrow from its notch on his bow.

"Eliza, what are you doing?" Caleb exclaimed.

"This man made a mistake and is now fighting for his life. Extend him the same courtesy as you did before."

Caleb looked at her, took in a deep breath, and exhaled. "Cousin, you are…" he stopped talking and extended a long stick towards the swimmer. He couldn't finish his thought. It made no sense to him that she treated this man so well when he tried to harm her.

"Your mother taught this to me. Do you remember her stories of when Yeshua was approached by the Pharisees who were ready to stone to death a man who had committed a sin?"

"Yeah," he said, only partly remembering what she was talking about.

"Yeshua said, 'Let the man who has no sin cast the first stone.' The Pharisees realized that none of them were sinless, and none threw any stones."

He was pierced by her words. Caleb had sinned. He took a deep breath and looked at her.

"I guess you're right." Caleb walked out and helped the man finish stepping out of the water and onto dry land. He acknowledged Caleb's help with a nod and walked towards the fire. Eliza moved aside and gave him her place out of the smoke but near the warmth.

"Bless you," he said, pausing only for a second to look Eliza in the eye. He sat down, shivering in his wet clothes, hoping to warm up and survive.

Eliza returned to her pack as she was warmed enough to move around comfortably. Although much of Eliza's pack remained soaked with salt water, the food remained edible. She offered everyone some of her dried meat and some soggy bread. While the three men ate, she quickly accounted for all the gold purses that were in the middle of the pack. They weighed more than anything else in her pack.

Caleb approached the last man to arrive. Although the man was nearing a state of hypothermia, Caleb's anger was not about to be restrained.

"My cousin spared your life, and I do not know how. You deserve to die. You know that, right?"

The man nodded, but the shame he felt prevented him from looking Caleb in the eye. He began to cry, first slowly, then without abandon.

"What are you doing that for? Stop crying!" the deck-hand chided. "These folks let you live when no one else in the world would have. Did you see the ring he wears? That is the ring of a ruthless sort of man. No legate would let a crime like yours go unpunished. You are...well, I do not know what you are, other than lucky to be alive." The man stopped his crying and only stared straight ahead into the fire.

Caleb got up and left to go into the woods, feeling nothing but anger that Eliza was so quick to forgive this villain. Eliza watched the event transpire, and she considered following after him, but she let him go. He came back a few moments later, having composed himself. He brought a large bundle of wood and dropped it next to the fire before speaking.

"There is a stream for fresh water, and there is lots of wood to burn in the forest. We will need to stay here tonight and come up with a plan in the morning. We will need to get some wood for the fire and keep it stoked during the night." He intentionally walked towards Eliza and stood near her. His intent to protect her was obvious.

For most of the afternoon, the deckhand told stories of his two other shipwrecks. He talked about the Egyptians, the Galls, the Saxons, and just about everyone else other than his own family and friends. And they all talked about the captain. As the sun began to set, the fatigue of the day's stress began to set in, and all of them were ready to sleep before the sun had fully set.

"My cousin is sleeping all night, and the three of us will take a watch," Caleb announced. "I will take my watch first while she sleeps. The rest of you can sleep once you gather more wood. You have my word: I will not slit your throats while you sleep unless you fail to get up and get some wood right now."

"Enough of acting like the tough guy," Eliza said to him in guttural Hebrew. "We need to act like we were raised, for no other reason than to honor our family." The men were fearful of Caleb, and they immediately stood up to retrieve their share of the needed firewood from the forest.

"Please wait for a moment. What are your names?" she asked the two men.

"I am called Balbinus," said the man who had tried to rape her. "People call me Balbi."

"And I am Priscus," said the deckhand.

"Well, good. Balbi and Priscus, I am going to sleep. We are all lucky to be alive, aren't we?"

"Yes," they both said simultaneously.

"My name is Eliza, by the way. I am the daughter of Matthew and Katya from the Hebrew village of Correae. By Roman law, each of you is required to serve us until we release you, as we have saved your lives from an act of the gods."

Both men paused and looked at each other. By law, they were her slaves, now. They knew it.

"Yes, that is the rule," said Balbi. "Whatever you say, we will do."

"For now, I have not told you of our plans, but tomorrow, you will help us get back on the way to Rome."

"How do you propose we do that?" Priscus asked.

"Just wait until tomorrow," she said.

Caleb spoke to her in Hebrew once she was finished. "And you think I take risks! Ha! You just added a known criminal to our lot and a man we knew nearly nothing about."

She replied in Greek, so all could hear. "Yeshua added disciples before they were old enough to be worth even half their weight. And they changed the world. We are going to need help, as we do not know where we are going, and we won't know our way around Rome when we do get there."

Caleb thought he saw his mother in Eliza. That is how she would have handled the situation.

Caleb took a deep breath. "Good night, Cousin," was all he could say. The men soon returned, and they all watched in silence at the last of sunset in the west. Eliza lay inside her sleeping blanket not far from the fire while all the men stood around the fire, as they could not yet fall asleep. Priscus spoke next.

"My boat and my captain are gone," looking now only into the fire. Everyone nodded. They were all starting to feel that loss.

Balbi turned towards Eliza as she was sitting up in her bedroll, looking at the dance inside of the flames.

"Thank you for saving my life," he said, using a most contrite tone. "I will do what you ask," he continued, bowing his head and turning back to the fire. "You are more of a woman than any I have known," he added, still staring at the fire. Those words prompted a small but inaudible snort from Caleb that he hoped no one heard. But they all did.

Eliza leaned back and quickly fell asleep. The two others joined her, and Caleb told Balbi he would wake him in a few hours. Caleb sat near the fire but out of the line of smoke and watched Eliza sleep as he had done several times before. He witnessed her dreaming and her occasional talking, but he couldn't tell who she was talking to. Was she battling some demons? He wondered if she were reliving the attempted rape or if it was something about her parents. She was obviously tormented by something.

It reminded him of what she referenced earlier with one of his school lessons. There was nothing in the real world she was battling when she slept—all her battles were now in her mind. But how did it get into her mind?

"Yeshua, strengthen my cousin now, as she battles her demons. Remind her that You are there with her, in all things," were Caleb's prayer.

Eliza sat up, nearly panting. Caleb saw her face in the light from the fireplace, and she was tormented.

"You were having a bad dream. Go back to sleep. You are safe now," he said.

"Okay," she said, pulling the bedroll up to her chin. She let her eyes close, and she fell back asleep.

Caleb woke up Balbi and started his night's sleep, laying where Balbi had been. He placed his sword inside his bedroll as he nodded at Balbi. Balbi closed his eyes as he acknowledged the expectation his new masters had on him to keep the watch in the middle of the night to keep them all safe. Caleb stared at Balbi before saying his final prayers, asking God to remove the bitterness he had towards Balbi.

The rest of the night passed without any events.

RE-ENTERING CIVILIZATION

Priscus had the last watch before sunrise and had already stoked the fire when everyone else woke up. Winter meant shorter days, and they all had a full night's sleep. The warm fire and an uneventful night allowed them the happiness of waking up rested. Priscus was obviously lonely, and he started a conversation with Caleb and Eliza as soon as they started moving.

"I wasn't paying that great of attention, but I am pretty sure that there is a Roman fishing village called Reggio up the coast. I bet it is less than a quarter day's walk. We ought to go there."

"Agreed," Caleb said in a groggy state. "Staying here and waiting for someone to come to get us is not the best idea. Eliza, what do we have to eat?"

She sat up on her knees and took a deep breath before answering him.

"We have more dried meat, but we are out of oranges and nearly out of water." She stood up and walked a few steps towards her backpack. She reached in and took out what she had, serving everyone else before taking any for herself.

Everyone was grateful to be alive; food in their stomachs was a benefit they weren't expecting.

Since Caleb and Eliza were the only ones with any of their stuff intact after the shipwreck, everyone watched as the two Hebrews packed. Caleb was grateful that a lot of his stuff had dried out overnight. His bedroll still had some moisture in it, but everything else was dry. As he was putting on his pack, Eliza looked at Priscus and spoke up.

"Let's go towards…what did you call it?"

"Reggio!"

They began walking up the coast with Caleb, the tracker, in the front. After a short while, Caleb stopped and pointed them to go inland. After entering the forest, he bent down on one knee and stopped everyone to talk to them.

"This is a trail that runs parallel to the shore in both directions. You can see all the prints on the ground here. If we take it north, we are sure to come up to Reggio. Follow me, but do not talk." He did not wait for an answer before walking. He stopped them after a brief while and knelt on one knee again. "I have been seeing human footprints for a while, but now we have livestock markings. We are close to something."

By mid-morning, they began hearing the sounds of metal striking a rock ahead of them. Soon, some manmade structures appeared, and there was a village with about thirty to fifty houses ahead of them. They could see the blacksmith's shack ahead of them, obviously the source of the noises they heard in the forest.

"Yeah, this is it," said Priscus. "I've sailed by this place too many times to count but haven't stopped here in years. You cannot miss that big red roof over there." He pointed to a two-story inn that had been painted red. "We will find everything we need around there." He stepped ahead of everyone and walked into the village.

"Priscus, I am already glad you are with us," Eliza declared. "Can you find two rooms for us at a dockside inn and start negotiating seats on a boat to Rome?"

"Yes, Ms. Eliza. I am on it. You guys can go to the village center. I will come and find you after I talk to the dockmaster." He walked away, and Balbi followed him.

This hamlet had a unique blend of greenery and seafront, a geography unknown anywhere in ancient Judah. Caleb had not seen some of these varieties of trees before, either. Eliza had no interest in a conversation about treescapes, but she also was not going to leave Caleb's side.

"Do you think we can talk and walk at the same time?" she asked in her playful tone.

"After you!" Caleb said, pointing forward with his hand. Caleb's hunger got the best of him, and he headed straight for the tavern at the center of town. On the way, she entered the market. She stopped Caleb to engage some of the shopkeepers before their two new slaves returned. She knew that they were close to Rome, and she had no idea what Roman fashion or Roman cuisine looked like. After all, she was in another country for the first time in her life, and everything seemed exciting. She all but forgot that she was shipwrecked yesterday. She did what she always did, surveying the vendors and shoppers in the market, looking for those engaged in larger buying or selling operations. She engaged them in conversation, trying to casually inquire about the price of cinnamon here. She was still carrying a lot of it, though it was a bit wet. When they told her its worth, she responded with absolutely no body language and thanked them for their help. Caleb reminded her of his hunger, and they continued traveling towards the inn. Once they were out of hearing range, she turned and whispered.

"Our cinnamon is worth nearly three times as much as when we had bought it back home!" she said, unable to hold back her smile.

Priscus and Balbi walked up behind them as they arrived at the two-story inn and tavern.

"Talked to the dockmaster, and it turns out we know some of the same people," said Priscus. He, too, was smiling.

The act of re-entering civilization had revitalized all of them. Balbi's shame from attempting to rape Eliza was fading, and he was able to look at the two young Hebrews and speak.

"This place will have everything any of us need," Balbi said.

"What did you discover?" Eliza asked Priscus.

"My captain was rescued, as were some of the others on the boat, and they will be continuing to travel to Rome as soon as they can. The local synagogue has put them up. Apparently, they have an outreach for people stranded in the middle of their sea passage, offering food and lodging in exchange for labor. Unfortunately, young masters, there is nothing going to Rome today, but there is a vessel leaving tomorrow morning going straight to Rome, and you now have first-class seats."

"Well done," Eliza said with sincerity. "Let's celebrate with a meal. I have some questions."

They walked into the inn using the double doors in the front side that faced the market. It was relatively empty, as most people were still working or trading in the markets this time of day. The server approached them, telling them to sit anywhere. Without asking, he brought out four clay mugs of ale, but Eliza politely declined for all of them. Instead, she got them to bring out some of the soup that they already been cooking since mid-morning. It was hot and tasted wonderful. Everyone had two bowls before the server engaged them in conversation.

After a few moments of chatter, the server asked them a question. "Would you like to join us tonight at the synagogue? We are talking about the prophet Isaiah and his prediction of the Messiah. They came true, you know?"

Caleb looked up at the server and agreed that they would all come.

Little did they know what impact their attendance would have.

A Sinner Meets
a Savior

Eliza got all of her questions answered by Priscus before the mid-day meal was finished. In addition, their server reaffirmed that they were three days from Rome, and the ship that they reserved space on served only soup. What was it with soup in this part of the world?

The server also told them that the seas by the coast of Rome were a bit unpredictable in the winter, so no one ever looked forward to traveling on what could be rough and windy seas. That might be why they so readily found first-class tickets less than a day before sailing. The anxiety of rough seas overcame Eliza, again, and she responded by purchasing a second cloak for herself, made of Egyptian cotton. It was the warmest garment she had ever worn. Caleb, for his part, was happy with what he already had to wear, as all of his gear that was wet when they reached shore had now dried. Eliza knew how upset Caleb might get if she bought him new clothing, so she left him alone as she shopped.

They had an afternoon on the dry and non-moving ground, and they spent it together. The sun was bright, and the air was dry, so Caleb and Eliza set out their wet cinnamon sticks on some rocks in a clearing off the trail they had used to walk into the village. They told Balbi to watch it and, when it dried, to repack it in their bags. They left him and wandered the town for no other reason than to wander. They both laughed at how easy it was to walk on the ground compared to the deck of a moving ship.

That evening, as the sun began to set, their server from earlier found all four of them sitting by the docks. "I am glad that I found you. Let me introduce myself now that I am no longer at work." He was not a native Greek speaker, and everyone in the group was curious as to what he called home, but he never volunteered.

"My name is Avi. Our synagogue is a short walk north from the port up that hillside." He pointed to the top of a partially blocked hill.

"There is only one trail leading up the hill. Come! Follow me." He began walking towards the path.

Caleb knew from his father's teachings that getting people to follow someone only required one person to be enthusiastically responsive. Despite not wanting to sit through a revival celebration, Caleb quickly stood up and followed Avi up the hill. He knew this evening was more for Balbi and Priscus than him and his cousin. Everyone followed Avi and Caleb, as he knew they would.

Avi had run ahead of them and was waiting for them when they got to the entrance to the synagogue, holding plates of warm bread, hummus, and dried fish. There were others like him, also offering food to those who were arriving, and there were ornate tables outside of the entrance where everyone was sitting and eating their meal.

"These people remind me a lot of the people back home at my synagogue," Caleb observed. "They come here to eat. I remember that Yeshua and His disciples used free food more than once to bring together a group to teach them. Hopefully, we will get some teaching tonight."

Eliza had always been spiritually bold, and she spoke with an authority that seemed strange from someone who was nearly raped and drowned in the same week. "This is a gift from Yahweh, not only that we are alive and safe, but that we are warm and have full stomachs. This is a far cry from when we were swimming for our lives, isn't it?"

"Yes, Ms. Eliza," said both Priscus and Balbi. Now that each man was indebted to her, they spoke to her more like slaves did than did men many years her senior.

As the sky turned deep red and the meal concluded, the rabbi came out from inside the temple carrying a lamp. He turned to everyone and called them inside, reminding them not to bring any food in with them and take off their sandals upon entry.

As Caleb and Eliza approached, the rabbi stopped them. "Aren't you Mishi's boy?" he asked Caleb.

"I am," Caleb responded. He knew what was coming next. The rabbis in the house of healing had prepared them for such questions.

"How are you parents, son?"

"My father and mother were killed by Roman soldiers about two weeks ago," he said, looking the rabbi in the eyes.

"I am sorry for your loss," the rabbi replied thoughtfully.

"Thank you very much. Please pray for us all. That will help us."

Caleb and Eliza had been instructed not to make their parent's murder into a drawn-out affair. Even though this man knew Caleb's parents, he was still a stranger and not some long-awaited friend. This was not the moment to discuss their whole story.

The rabbi greeted many others as they entered, placing his hand on their foreheads, blessing them in the Hebrew tradition. As a woman, Eliza expected no such blessing since tradition prevented male and female touching in public unless they were immediate family. She attempted to walk past the rabbi unobtrusively, but he touched her forehead anyway, offering her the same blessing as the men. She fell into the single-file line, just as everyone else did, but she was completely stunned by another instance of cultural and moral boundary-crossing. The rules of their faith did also not apply in Reggio, either.

"Caleb, these people aren't like us, but they know the same Yeshua that we do. This is weird," she said.

She decided that this man must have been impacted by her aunt's teachings of Yeshua. Yeshua did not come only for the Jews but for every man and woman. She remembered how passionate her aunt would become as she taught this message, reading from the Scriptures she had helped to transcribe. This man must have either heard or read these teachings.

That evening, the rabbi shared a story of his recent trip to Rome to visit several men in prison who used to be members of a group he knew and loved. He told everyone that they were being well taken care of by the local ministry, never wanting for food or provisions. He also shared that one of the prison guards had become a Yeshuaian. The rabbi told them he had traveled one evening with the guard to their underground synagogue and saw great acts of God's grace, despite the structure existing within walking distance of the Roman Senate and center of commerce. He ended the evening by calling anyone who had not yet believed the message of Yeshua's resurrection to come forward and profess their faith.

Before he could finish his alter call, Balbi went forward to receive the gifts presented by the rabbi. The rabbi greeted him and spoke loud enough for all to hear.

"Do you accept that you are a sinner and that you need a Redeemer to be right with Yahweh?" the rabbi asked.

Balbi looked up at the rabbi as a boy might look at his father when he was caught stealing a loaf of bread from a neighbor. "Yes," he said timidly.

"Do you accept the forgiveness of sins that our Messiah offers you, promising to give your life to Him and to serve Him?"

"Yes," he said, this a bit more loudly.

"Just as John the Baptist did for many years ago, I baptize you with water to symbolize your commitment to Yahweh. Yahweh extends His mercy to you that you may have eternal life. Go forth, Balbi." The rabbi took a small container of water and poured it on Balbi's head. The congregation began to cheer and clap. Balbi was amazed by the applause. He rubbed the water from his eyes before raising his hands to the sky, asking, "Am I saved yet?" The congregation both laughed and applauded again, affirming his public profession of faith.

Caleb shook his head and exhaled a single shallow breath with force.

"Had I killed that man, this day would have never come," he whispered to Eliza. She looked him in the eyes and nodded, then she rested her head on his chest for the moment.

"He would have missed it," Caleb elaborated the point, using simple words that meant something more to him.

For her part, Eliza was realizing that she needed to validate her cousin if they were going to complete this trip to Rome, meet the emperor and return to Judah without dying.

She thoughtfully wrapped her arms around him. "Cousin, you know I love you," she said.

Those were the words of affirmation that the teenage boy needed. He closed his eyes and smiled, thanking the Messiah not only for Balbi by also for the gift of his cousin. Caleb bent his chin down, kissing the top of Eliza's head, rubbing it as he knew she liked. They released after a moment when the congregation began to leave. They politely shared Hebrew goodbyes with others in attendance, noting how few knew to say *kol tuv* at the end of a ceremony in the synagogue.

They waited outside for Balbi and Priscus to join them. They walked back to the inn, listening to Balbi tell stories of his past without interruption. Once they made it to the inn, Priscus and Balbi retired to their rooms, as did Caleb and Eliza. With only a candle to light their room, Eliza and Caleb spoke about what lay ahead of them.

"Tomorrow we leave, and in three days, we will be in Rome," Eliza mused with a sense of wonder. "Caleb, how are we going to get to speak with the emperor once we get there?"

"I do not know, but we will find help. I am sure of it. That is part of my faith, Eliza. I do not need to know in advance. I need only courage in the present. Why else do you think I like to hunt?"

She had no response that included words, but she felt incomplete and small in a way that she hadn't felt since she ran away from her parents when they were in shackles for a trip that she did not know they were taking. Caleb had something that she did not. He had peace about the future in a way that made her jealous.

Caleb did not wait. He blew out the candle and told her to go to sleep. He said a final prayer himself before closing his eyes. "Lord, thank you for not letting me kill that man. I know he deserved it, but he deserved what happened tonight even more. Please forgive me of my crimes in the same way you forgave Balbi of his crimes. Amen."

Eliza had her own prayer.

"Great Jehovah Jireh. Please give me places to be courageous like my cousin. When they come, please give me awareness that they are upon me and teach me to be like Caleb. Amen."

VISIONS OF BRAVERY

Caleb was awake and moving long before Eliza. When she finally woke up and started packing, Caleb returned to the room and joined her, as they both had a boat to catch.

"Hey, I was down at the docks looking at our new ride. I saw the old captain, and he is safe and wishes us well."

"Really? Wow, that is great!" she said. Caleb continued with some smaller conversation, but one sentence stood out above the others.

"You know, half that boat was full of women, and you were the only one to survive the wreck," he said, without looking up as he stowed his bedroll on the bottom of his pack. He also carefully stowed the sheep bladders that saved their lives just two days ago.

Eliza had a pause in her packing as she remembered one of her aunt's teachings. After hearing Caleb's words, her teachings made sense for the first time.

"Prayer is timeless. God hears all of our prayers. It is when we say them that we know they are prayers. I tell you now there will be times in your life when you pray for something only to realize that you already had it. It was the act of praying that brought it to your attention."

She decided she needed to hear his opinion before drawing any conclusions.

"Caleb, this is a serious question, so no dumb answers," she said, trying to be authoritative. Caleb did not stop to look at her but continued inspecting the bladders for leaks or small holes.

"Do you think it was courageous to jump off the boat and swim to shore?" she asked with timidity.

Caleb paused, but he still did not look at her.

"Some. It was common sense, too. The boat was not going to float much longer, and we needed to get off of it to survive. But, yeah, it was brave, especially for you or someone like you," he said. That wasn't exactly a perfect answer, but it did make her feel brave.

She nodded her head, causing Caleb to ask her why.

"Well, when I prayed last night, I asked for Jehovah Jireh to give me bravery under duress like you have," she said. Caleb set down the bladder and crossed the room to where her wooden framed bed sat in the corner.

"Cousin, it is my job to be brave for you, and for both of us, really. You are brave, but not in the same way that I am. God has made us man and woman, and we do not have the same calling. My mom and dad were both ridiculously brave people, even up to the minute that they died, I suspect, but it wasn't the same kind of bravery. You know, of all things in this world, you need not worry about having too much gold and bravery," he said, kissing her on the forehead and walking back to packing.

That is what she needed. His affirmation meant something to her.

VISIONS OF ROME

The walk from the inn to the docks was quick, even adding time to stop and buy fresh bread in the market. Even though this portside village was small, its port was deep. That meant they needed smaller docks than the ones in Joppa. It also reduced loading and unloading time. The path down to the water was surrounded by trees, and they were surprised to find the rabbi waiting at the docks for them.

Before they boarded the ship, the rabbi blessed Balbi again, and he graciously received it. He wished the new Yeshuaian good travels. However, he kept both Caleb and Eliza at his side, asking them to spend a moment with him alone.

For his part, Priscus had been released from his debt to return to help his captain. Both Caleb and Eliza thought the man had more to offer his captain than he would ever offer them. The company he and the captain worked for owned a network of ships, and Priscus would be put into a rotation to sail other vessels between locations after a brief period of administrative work. They may even see him again. They decided that Balbi would be the only one accompanying them to Rome.

Caleb asked Balbi to take their gear into the boat, and the rabbi began speaking to the children quietly in Hebrew.

"On our journey through life, we are taught that we each have a moment when a part of our story seems bigger than our whole life. I had a vision for you two that I must share with you. I see your next steps will be bigger than your lives."

They had both heard Mishi say similar things in the past. They both listened closely to the Hebrew leader's next words.

He adjusted his robe, as he was accustomed to, and began rocking back and forth. Displaying his mild obesity without shame, he raised his hands and closed his eyes as he spoke. His voice cracked, as it often did when visions given by Elohim were spoken in public. He hummed for a moment, then he started sharing.

"I saw a scroll being written, and the scroll was the story of your family's lives. The first pages included the story of both of your parents, and the last pages included only your story. The writer of the scroll was surrounded by two angels, one on each side of him, and each one was looking at the page while he wrote. Above the three, there were many birds flying. Behind him, there was a rainbow containing more colors than I can express. The author had run out of paper and was tempted to end the story, but the angels shook their heads when he attempted to stop. Instead, the birds provided him with additional parchment, and he continued on a new sheet with new words of new tales. These were your tales! Moments later, his quill ran out of ink, and, again, he wanted to stop. This time, the angels provided him with more ink, and with each writing, the ink became more purple, a sign of ever-increasing royalty. He smiled greatly as he wrote the story, and he wrote it quickly as if he could barely keep up with the words."

Eliza opened her mouth, about to speak, but no words came out. She looked at Caleb.

The rabbi lowered his hands and opened his eyes. He put his hand on their shoulders. "Little ones, I have no knowledge of what you are doing in Rome. Your parents' death has grieved us all. Yet I can see that your life is soon to become royal, although I do not know how."

Finally, words came to Eliza. "Really? Is there anything in your dream about what it is that we do?"

"I see the two of you before a great throne, opening your hands and extending a gift to a man who sits on that throne. I do not know who he is, nor do I know what the gift might be. I have asked Elohim to show me what the man on the throne gives you, but I have not understood the image. It appears that he extends back to you what you gave him, but it now contains both confidence and power."

"What do you mean you do not understand the image?" asked Caleb, a bit perplexed.

"It appears that he dismisses you, but you do not leave, and that is connected to the gift."

The two Hebrews looked at each other, checking if the other understood the message. They were equally perplexed.

"Thank you, teacher," Eliza said earnestly. "That gives me some courage."

"How is that?" asked the rabbi in a curious tone.

"I will tell you our story so far," said Caleb. Caleb put his arm around Eliza and pulled her in close to himself, and they had walked towards a more secluded spot off the pier. Caleb had finally decided that this man was trustworthy. He paused for a moment, then he told the rabbi what had happened since Eliza had arrived in Tamar a few weeks ago.

"You two are full of surprises. I am beginning to see what the writer in my dreams was recording."

Caleb and Eliza saw their new captain standing at the top of the plank, looking for his missing passengers. "We have to go now, rabbi," said Eliza. Before leaving, Caleb reached into the stash of Eliza's village's coins, and he went to give one small bag of them to the rabbi. He looked Eliza in the eye, checking for her approval before handing the man the coins. She nodded.

"May the Messiah remain alive and well in your community. May this wealth help you do that." He used words that he had heard his father use.

"Young man, you sound like your father, even if you do not really look like him," said the rabbi. Caleb wanted to hide his face but paused. This would not be a good moment to tell the rabbi that he was not biologically his father's son.

"You might want to try to stop killing Romans, especially if you need their help," said the rabbi with a chuckle.

They smiled and stepped onto the deck of the heavy wooden sailing ship, pausing only briefly to turn around and wave the chubby rabbi farewell. As they went below decks to visit their home for the next three days, they saw Balbi.

"I will guard your stuff, little masters. I will protect it with my life, as you have spared mine, twice."

"Thank you, Balbi," said Eliza. She chose to believe that Balbi would never be a problem to them again. They climbed the steps from the lower deck to the top deck and walked to the front of the boat to watch the departure from there.

Soon, the land was too far away to swim to. Today's seas were not completely calm, but there was also no fear of capsizing. The sky was clear, with no clouds in sight, and the low humidity of the winter breeze felt relaxing.

"Ahead of us are the straits of Messene," said the captain, "with a long history of humbling watercraft and crew. We are going to take this vessel right through the middle because that is where it is safest."

"He'll get no argument from me!" said the passenger standing behind Eliza. The children turned around and greeted a young trader. After a few more moments, the captain finished his briefing, and everyone returned to the task of being a passenger.

"So, are you on your way to Rome to make a small fortune for yourself?" As usual, Caleb was making assumptions as he spoke to the man who spoke up earlier.

"No. Not a chance. I am looking to make a big fortune!"

Caleb recognized the color on the man's robes and identified him as one of the surviving members of the Sadducees, a group that had wielded great power in old Jerusalem before the Temple was destroyed. The Sadducees were responsible for maintaining the Temple, and there were several families of them next to his grandparents and father when he was a boy attending the Temple Mount school. Although the color was no longer identified by the current generation as that of a Sadducee, Caleb took the risk of his assumption. He had seen his father take such non-verbal risks in the past and felt no fear of failure.

All the students at their school learned that when the Temple fell, the Sadducees were blamed for failing to protect it, and their leaders were publicly stoned by the very stones that made up the Temple. The surviving members of their sect fled and scattered around Judah. Many mainstream members of the Hebrew nation considered them to be traitors and failures before God, having not protected Herod's Second Temple as they had vowed to. Now, only individual families remained, and many of them had become merchants, bartering both with Romans and Hebrews and initiating commerce between both parties.

"Did you enjoy the stop in that town back there?" the trader asked. "Do not remember seeing you on the boat out of Joppa. Were you on a different boat?"

"We were," said Eliza. She grabbed Caleb's arm, knowing that her cousin was prone to saying too much if she did not jump into the conversation. "We came here only a day or so earlier on a different boat. We visited the synagogue and spoke with the rabbi there for some time. Did you get to attend any of the services there?"

"I did not. We were only in that little port town for less than a day, and I did not want to. People can be mean, you know?"

Caleb read correctly.

"You know, the synagogue experience is unique now, especially for those of us who have had an experience with the Messiah. It is so wonderful to be rid of the burdens placed on us by the sins of our past." Caleb continued.

"When the Messiah appeared, everyone thought that He was coming to save us from the oppression of Roman occupation, in the same way that Yahweh saved our ancestors from Pharaoh and Nebuchadnezzar. But He was not here to repeat what His Father had done. He came to fulfill Yahweh's promises that we learned in the scrolls of Isaiah."

"You are not the first person to tell me this," the trader said, staring into the distance.

"What did you hear before?" asked Eliza.

"What you said. But there were more words used."

"Did you consider what you heard by comparing it to the ancient scrolls? A man of your stature must surely be able to read and write in our sacred language."

"No, I did not. I am proud of my family, and I do not want to shame them."

"You know, my parents were teachers of the ancient scrolls and of the message of the Messiah. I know that you are a descendant of a Sadducee family, and you are loved by Yeshua just as much as any Hebrew. That is the message of the sacred scrolls, now that they are complete," Caleb said, pausing long enough for the words to germinate.

Eliza continued speaking and teaching most boldly for a female Hebrew to ever talk to a male.

"The Temple had to fall for the prophecies of Isaiah to come to pass. It was not your family's fault that the Temple fell, no matter how mean people have been to you. Yahweh required that this event occur to show the world that His Son was here," she said, standing close to Caleb.

The man lifted his chin and stared straight ahead. He was formulating words to attach to his thoughts, and they came out slowly. He did not know how to process that he was standing with others who knew of his family history yet were not condemning or scorning him. This was rare, indeed. He spoke slowly.

"My parents were good people. We all had to leave Jerusalem quickly when the Temple fell. We had to take up a disguise to avoid people from stoning us to death for dereliction of duty to the Jewish state," he shared. Caleb held his own chin and nodded, prompting the man to continue.

"What could my parents really have done to stop any of that? My father was an accountant for the Temple and the Temple school. Those two behemoths that walked up the hill and into the city walls could not have been stopped by any Jews," he said with a rhetoric question that he obviously had lingering in his heart for far too long.

Caleb knew a bit of humility and humor would help all of them through this moment. At least, that was what he was taught.

"My father said they smelled bad and were very noisy animals, as well. Those animals were really the conquerors, weren't they?" he said.

For the rest of the day, Eliza explained to the Sadducee the full tale of Yeshua and His message, using the writings from the sacred scrolls that her aunt had taught her. The young man reciprocated with equal openness and shared many tales of his youth when his family had fled Jerusalem nearly fourteen years ago when he was only nine years old. He asked her some questions, most of which she could either not answer or only partially answer. Soon, the sun was ready to set, and both of them were hungry as they had spent the day on the outside on the deck. Eliza was grateful that she had purchased the extra cloak and scarf. For his part, Caleb and the Sadducee looked a bit sunburned.

"So, now that we have shared this with you, what do you feel in your heart?" asked Eliza. "Do you believe it possible that Yeshua fulfilled the Scripture of our ancestors and was the Messiah?" This was the question that she had been taught to ask once she had finished telling her stories. Her aunt had told her one day at dinner that when she would tell the story of Yeshua and ask someone if they thought it was true, she would hear a unique song in her soul. Eliza had never understood what her aunt meant until that moment. A resonance in her soul started as she shared with this man and asked him if he believed.

One of her aunt's teaching came to life, and Eliza could hear her aunt talking to her as she spoke.

"Eliza, it is only your job to ask; it is the listener's job to accept or refuse. The difference between these people's jobs must not be confused," she would teach. Yael learned early in her ministry to let go of expectations that any man would accept Yeshua based on her words. She needed only to share the words and the teachers, then let Yeshua do the work.

"You know, I think so. Yes, my family were sinners, and I am a sinner, as well. I can see your point that we all are sinners and in need of a Savior. This idea that you suggest that He came to save us from our sin and not from the Romans…well, I do not know what it is. But it is beautiful." He began to laugh, and a single tear flowed from his eye. He was shamed and quickly wiped it away.

"Even followers of The Way, as we used to be called, need to eat," said Caleb, breaking the tension. "Let's go get some food, since it looks like you are one of us, now." Caleb walked up and put his left arm around the man and his right arm around Eliza, and they walked towards the passenger kitchen and an unending bowl of soup that was awaiting them every day for the next three days. Eliza appreciated that this man knew of their cultural boundaries and did not try to touch her. In Hebrew culture, she would never touch this man in public until they had completed *erusin* and committed publicly to marry. However, it was perfectly normal for Caleb to embrace the man and to embrace her. It felt good to feel safe.

"Yes, I am one of you, I believe," he shared as they started walking.

Eliza had never been given an opportunity to lead another Jew to Yeshua before this moment. She had seen both her aunt and uncle do it, but she had never seen her parents do it, as nearly everyone in Correae was already of Yeshuaian belief. The resonance was now loud, and she felt enriched.

The man reached into his royal robes, pulled out a purse of coin, and handed it to them. "Please take this for what you shared with me today."

Eliza raised her hand and refused his offering. Instead, she quoted a portion of the Torah to him. "During the Exodus, the Lord said to Moses, 'Tell the Jews to bring Me an offering. You are to receive the offering for me from everyone whose heart prompts them to give.' It's obvious that you have been prompted to give. However, please save this to give to one of our underground synagogues in Rome. We have been taught that the underground synagogues are growing, and they need all the help that they can get." He bowed, a sign that he agreed to their conditions.

"I will do that," he said.

They all ate dinner together, talking with other passengers during the meal. They asked everyone why they were traveling to Rome. There were many who had brought cargo with them to trade. However, some had come for education. Some were returning from visits abroad. Some were going to work in the city's public works projects, and some were there to relieve family who had finished a four-month shift on service in Thessalonica and were getting a break. Rome was a melting pot of all the world's cultures and trades unlike any place in Judah, including Jerusalem, and this boat's passengers reflected that diversity.

After they finished traversing the straits of Messene, the captain yelled down to everyone from the deck. "We have seen the worst of the currents for the day. We will ride the shore to your right and to the east, all the way to Rome. Sleep well. This shall be an easy journey, now."

The trader gave Caleb a warm embrace. "Thank you for restoring my family's honor. They never accepted the loss of their dignity when the Temple fell. I will tell them of Yeshua and show them the same words of the Torah that you showed me, and I pray that they will rest better."

After Caleb and Eliza went below deck, they dismissed Balbi to go above deck to get some food and see the sunset.

It was just as the captain said. They arrived well-rested in Rome early on the fourth day.

AFTER THE FIRE

As the boat entered the mouth of the Tiber river, there were multiple harbors from which to dock the watercraft. The most important port was Ostia, but the new and preferred port at Portus was filled with slaving vessels, nearly all coming in from Africa to the south and uncivilized lands to the west. It was clear that the city had been damaged by a fire, as some of the docks were burned and unusable. The captain sailed past many ships waiting to dock at Portus, and the scenes on the decks of those ships were unlike anything that either Caleb or Eliza had heard of.

The decks of at least half of the boats were filled with dark-skinned Egyptian men and women. The slaves were all chained together, and they were talking out loud in an unknown language. Most were barely clothed and appeared to be freezing, angry, or both. The voices were loud, and anytime any of them made a move, they would get whipped. Eliza turned her head at the violence. Once they passed the last of the slave ships, they entered the section of the port meant for citizen passenger services. Their boat slowed to a near crawl, and they were within a rope's throw from their dock when Eliza started asking Balbi some questions.

"What were they saying?"

"They want to know what they are going to do in the city. The man on the shore said they are going to help rebuild the city since the fire."

"Fire? What caused it?" asked Eliza.

"It's been a year, but it was really bad. When I first came here, it was still burning, although the city was open for business. You know the Romans." Rome was notorious for allowing commerce to continue in an unfettered state, no matter the needs of the poor.

"But what caused it?" she repeated.

"Some people said that the old emperor caused it. Some say that Yeshuaians started the fire. You know, there are a lot of them here now, and some people have a theory that they did it. I do not believe this claim, though. I do not know many Yeshuaians, but none of the ones that I know do things like that. Most people think it was just an accident. You go walking through the different regions of the city, and you can see that the Romans do not care about most of the people in this city who aren't Roman royalty. Slave quarters and housing for simple folks are close together, and it gets cold and windy in the winter. I think the wind caused a cooking fire to jump from house to house and quarter to quarter. One thing is for sure, though. This new emperor has spent a lot trying to rebuild things quickly. No matter who caused it, he is cleaning it up and rebuilding with purpose."

The children we so intent on listening to Balbi's story that they did not notice that they were next to unload.

Balbi continued. "The most important thing the new emperor did after the last of the fires were put out was to finish building the Colosseum for all the fighting that people around here love to see. That place is unique on all the earth!"

The boat hit the dock. Men from the port immediately jumped onto the boat's main deck, going directly to the captain, looking forward to collecting docking fees and get a copy of the written manifest showing who was on the boat and how much weight in goods they were carrying. They charged a tax per head on board and a tax per human weight of gear, and it was the captain's job to pay that sum before anyone or any goods could leave the vessel. To make sure, four Roman soldiers dressed in the most exquisite of armor stood next to the plank, holding javelins in their hands, awaiting the word to allow passengers and cargo exit. Or to kill them. During that moment, everyone's fate was in the hands of the captain's ability to hand over gold and silver.

The captain gave them the required coins, and the Roman in charge said, "Welcome home, my friends," in open Greek.

Caleb picked up his stuff and told Balbi to get the rest. He exhaled once and turned to Eliza.

"The time for talk about how to get to Rome and see the emperor is now complete. Now that we are here, we need to go to him. Let's go, Cousin."

Finding What Was Right in Front of You

The trader who they had met on the boat left quickly, leaving the docks in a great hurry. "I know I will see you again," he said as he shuffled away. Eliza realized that she had never learned the man's name, and she felt ashamed.

"What is your name?" she called out.

He put his bags down and told both of his slaves to stop. "My name is Barkhi. 'Barkhi Hyrcanus of the Manasseh on the coast.' That's what we call ourselves when talking to others who are also in our sect."

"You are just Barkhi to us," said Caleb, as each man kissed each other on the cheek in keeping with Hebrew custom before departing.

In front of them stood the most glorious and diabolical place in the history of humans. It was finally time to explore it and find a way to get an audience with their uncle's childhood best friend. Balbi grabbed everyone's bags and found it amusing how awed Eliza and Caleb were by Rome. For first-time viewers, it was a mesmerizing sight.

"You two do not know what you are in for!" he said as he carried their bags off the boat.

But they were soon aghast at something that sat at the end of the docks where the Roman roads connected to them. There was a series of four wagons, each with a covered top with open sides. There were two women in each one, each wearing only an untied cloak and beautiful headdress. Each woman had men lined up, ready to please them. This was an open-air brothel, and neither of the children was prepared to see it.

"What are they doing?" asked Eliza, even though her mother had already told her exactly what was happening. These men had spent much time at sea, and as a reward for reaching Rome, they looked forward to a brief stop at these pleasure wagons. Neither Caleb nor Eliza could not stop staring at what they saw.

"You have never heard about this?" asked Balbi.

"I had heard that this happens, but I never believed it. Now I do," said Caleb. Caleb grabbed Eliza by her shoulder and turned her away from the wagons. "This is the evil that lies in the hearts of men that Solomon himself spoke about," he said to Eliza in the purest of Hebrew. She did not speak, but he felt her head nodding on his chest. He kissed her on the forehead and said, "Let's leave this place."

He whispered to her to keep her head down as they walked past the brothel wagons. As they got near to the wagons, every sound was now audible. Eliza began to cry under her breath, and Caleb could feel her heart beating rapidly as she passed what she thought might have become of her had she been raped and decided she was no longer worthy of marriage. She thought of what her aunt was able to endure and survive, and she did exactly what her aunt taught her to do: she prayed.

"Yeshua, please let there be a day when women do not mate in the streets like this, talking of filth and self-deprecation. Restore our people to Your moral code and redeem us," she said.

For his part, Caleb looked down almost exclusively at the road, but he, too, heard everything. He focused on the workmanship of the paths and roads that they were now walking on. The roads were exquisitely crafted with both stone and hewn brick in alternating color patterns. Some of the pathways that lead into Jerusalem and Hebron looked like this, but this was the first time that either of them had seen the "original" city that the roads and public works in ancient Judah were modeled after. Many of their families and friends were taught that God blessed the people of ancient Judah above all others. It took the teachings of Yael and Mishi to help them understand that the architectural achievements of Rome had long since dwarfed the greatest of Hebrew achievements.

As they passed by the last of the wagons and set a distance between themselves and the open-air brothel, Caleb released his grip on Eliza and allowed her to look up. They stood at the entrance to the world's largest commerce center—the place where the docks met the streets and markets. They walked one street removed from the road that paralleled the docks and stood in wonder at what lay before them.

At the center of each intersection was a piece of lapis lazuli. The blue rock was larger than a human head. "That one piece of stone in the middle of this road is worth as much as a parcel of land back home and the house that sits on it," Eliza exclaimed. The lavishness seemed unfathomable to the sense of financial stewardship. For her, the use of such a great amount of wealth for such a wasteful purpose was sinful.

"And to think that the horses just relieve their bowels on this beautiful stone," said Caleb, as they stood close together and walked up the hill. He saw a cylindrical container half as tall as a man on the intersection of the two paths. It was made of a pounded and thin silvery metal. "What is that?" he asked, walking towards it.

"That, young master, is a garbage can," said Balbi with a laugh.

"What is it for?"

"The Romans have decided that there should be no refuse discarded directly on the ground. Garbage of all sorts must be placed in these cans, and each night, they are emptied by slaves who carry the contents either to the river or to the great city burn pits."

"Caleb, look at how clean the streets here are!" Eliza said. She wasn't listening to Balbi.

"Huh," said Caleb, noticing for the first time that there was no refuse on the ground. "Is that why the rivers are so brown and dirty?" he asked Balbi.

"Hard to say, but that river is pretty much that color all year."

"My dad put something like this outside our town synagogue, but we did not use metal. Ours were made of clay, and the slaves there also emptied them twice a week. We would take turns going with our slaves to empty the pots," said Caleb.

"But the idea of doing that for everyone every day? That sounds crazy, but also wonderful!" Eliza added.

After walking uphill and away from the docks for a few hundred steps, they reached the crest of the hill. Ahead and downhill of them were more unknown structures and people, but first, they turned around and looked back from whence they came. The colors at the dockside seemed more vibrant now that they were distant from them, with brownish water and brown boats giving way to dark slaves, light-skinned Gauls, and colorful clothing on nearly everyone buying and selling. When combined with the noises of all the languages being spoken on the top of the hill, it felt like they were watching one of the plays that they would see in an amphitheater at the end of each school year.

Caleb was fascinated at the lines of slaves of all skin colors, steadily carrying items on their heads up the hill. He could not identify if the men in charge of the slaves were the buyers or the sellers of the merchandise, as they often spoke a language other than Greek. Many turned off the main route and took parallel side streets, and they would appear moments later, carrying nothing at all on their heads. It seemed like only moments later, they would reappear and climb up the hill with another load. It seemed like the lines of slaves never stopped. Balbi enjoyed the break from carrying the goods to let the two youth do some people watching. There were baskets made of reeds that only grow on the shores of the Nile, full of dolls for the rich children of the Roman nobility. There were small, human-drawn carts of bronze pots of all sizes and shapes. There were men wearing gloves carrying huge wheels of cheese with a smell unlike any they were familiar with. There was a large cart of pre-made torches being pulled by a huge horse. Caleb approached the cart and saw that the torches were soaked in a fluid that Caleb did not recognize. He learned from the vendor that they could burn all night and well into the next day before running out of the oil pre-soaked into them. It seemed like the parade of commerce might never end, but soon their hunger overtook their curiosity, and they all agreed to find some food. They saw a cart two streets away with a vendor selling fresh bread and some sort of thick soup, and they walked that way.

After they finished eating, Caleb wanted to walk to the Colosseum. It was the largest structure that now defined the heart of the city. Its walls seemed to be like that of a large egg, both oval in shape but with straight walls going upward into the sky. The walls wrapped around each other, and it appeared to lack any sort of roof. Caleb pointed to it and asked Balbi if that was it.

"Yes, it is. That structure is the new Colosseum, finished by Emperor Titus in his first year as emperor," Balbi said, with a sense of pride. "I have never been there, but I hear that it changes a man's soul to watch the events in there." He looked at the children and found it pleasing that they were enthralled by what their eyes saw now instead of the prostitution at the bottom of the hill.

"Tell us what happens in there," pleaded Eliza.

"They call them gladiator battles," said Balbi. He set down their bags and put his hands on his hips, looking up at the structure's immenseness.

"Keep going! Tell me more about the gladiator battles!" Caleb said.

"Well, Roman soldiers compete to see who the best fighter, but they do not always fight each other. Sometimes, they fight off great beasts and non-Romans, mostly slaves. When the battle starts, everyone watches them from above, and people cheer for who they want to win. The emperor watches every fight, and he decides if the battle must end in death or not. He usually gives a thumb-up sign, meaning fight to the death. Citizens like that the best." He lowered his voice and continued so no one could hear his next words. "This emperor really loves the combat, and he does some disturbing things. Sometimes he tells his soldiers to tie up or wound the opponents to make sure the best Roman soldiers win. Without meaning to, he makes folks cheer for the underdog in those moments. It is pretty sick if you ask me," said Balbi.

"I would be interested to see this!" said Caleb.

"And I would not!" added Eliza. Her breathing quickened. This was not a good morning to be a naive Jewish girl from Correae walking the streets of downtown Rome for the first time.

Their conversation ended abruptly as they heard a street crier. He walked near to them, speaking loudly. "Come! The Messiah has been on earth, and He offers forgiveness of sins! Come and meet Him!" He repeated his message about twice before moving to another spot, always looking around for people who might be listening to him.

Both Caleb and Eliza decided to approach the man. After all, he was one of them. As they began to walk that way, Balbi blocked them. "Do not engage this man. This is folly. The Romans will kill Yeshuaians on sight if they even think you are declaring someone as the Messiah ahead of the emperor. We have not come all this way to help you on your quest only to see you talking to a man out in public who can have you killed. I tell you this is folly!"

Caleb ignored him, stepping around him to the crier. "My name is Caleb," he said in Hebrew. "I wish to speak to your rabbi as soon as we can. Will you take us to him?" The man looked at Caleb curiously, but he did not reply. Caleb concluded that the man did not know any Hebrew. As such, he repeated what he said in Greek. "I know Yeshua, just as you do, and it is possible that your rabbi may be able to help us. Take me to him. We have a great need."

The man replied in Greek, as Caleb expected. "We meet each evening at sundown at the bottom of the Palatine Hill in the building with the yellow door. Continue down this hill in the direction that you have traveled. Knock on the yellow door, and you will be let in. If you wish to speak to the rabbi, come early. At present, the rabbi is working on the docks, as he is also a fisherman during the day." With that, the man left them and began uphill and away from the Colosseum and towards the docks. He repeated his message as he moved off.

"See there?" said Caleb, feeling successful in getting some information that might lead to an audience with the emperor. Eliza rolled her eyes and shook her head, almost like a disgusted wife. Caleb decided to ignore her attempt to downplay his success. "You two heard what he said? We have made the first step!" He dismissed Balbi for the rest of the day but told him to meet them at the yellow door, as instructed, before dinner.

A Carrot or
a Donkey?

Before speaking a single word to anyone, Eliza walked the
spice market from end to end, stopping to eavesdrop on conversations in progress. She heard that the Gauls were bringing in lots of wheat soon. There had been a flood during the
late autumn in Egypt, and some of their crop was lost, so the
Gauls would be getting a good price for their grain.

She was in her element when it came to navigating a
foreign market and negotiating the best value for her cinnamon. With no fear of her goods connecting back to the
gold ore of Correae, she spoke more openly than she otherwise would have. She introduced herself to several shopkeepers and negotiated fiercely for the best price. One shopkeeper attempted to offer her a below-market rate, and she
responded by pouring several gold coins from her purse and
counting them in front of him for no other reason than to
show that she knew how to value things. The man changed
his tone, offering her a much better price, but Eliza knew
others were watching their transaction, and she dismissed the
man and his efforts to lowball her. She knew that this dis-
carding of the man's newer offer would prevent others from
attempting to offer her a below-market price.

The largest shop in the market seemed to be staffed by entry-level workers, so she chose not to visit it. Experience taught her that they had a limit as to how high they could go in their offers. She suspected that she would not be able to negotiate above the number the owner had already authorized the shopkeeper to offer, making the large shops nearly worthless in larger transactions. The shop next door was not as large, but the owner was both present and approachable. Within a few minutes, she had emptied both her and her cousin's backpack of their cinnamon sticks and had taken possession of a large weight of newly minted Roman coins that had Titus' face on them.

"And that, my dear cousin, is how you do it," she said smugly, putting all the coins into a purse that she had just acquired. "That was enough profit to justify making this trip three times over." She told Caleb to follow her as they walked back towards the edge of the Colosseum, and she gave a few coins to beggars she had seen there earlier.

"Done yet?" Caleb asked, anxious to get back to meet the local rabbi.

"Yes," she replied. "It's moments like these that remind me of my purpose in the world and how I am supposed to use it to glorify God. We could have kept all those coins, but the beggars need them more than we do right now. And since we are here to help get my parents out, I needed to do something that they would be proud of."

Her justification gave Caleb a moment to pause. He took a few of her coins and gave them to the beggars as well, blessing them and praying for them just as he had seen his father do many times.

"I am glad you said that, Cousin. That would make my parents proud," said Caleb as they made their way directly to the yellow door. As they approached it, they saw that there was already someone there, also knocking to see the rabbi.

"Barkhi!" said Eliza.

"Hello," he said, bowing before them even though they were younger than he was, showing his respect for them publicly.

"You do not need to do that," said Eliza, feeling a bit bashful at his public display of honor.

The door opened, and a slave greeted them, asking them what their business was. Eliza did all the talking. "We just came from Judah, and we need the help of the rabbis at the local synagogue. We are friends and followers of The Way."

He closed the door. Within a few seconds, it was opened again by a different person who had a skeptical look about him. He wore a full beard and a rich head of long black hair, but his eyes were bloodshot as if he hadn't slept in days. "What is it that you want?"

Eliza had practiced her words for this moment. "We need to get an audience with the emperor. We are not asking for help with that, but we do need prayer. Does it not say, 'Where two or more are gathered in my name, there I am with them?'" Only a Yeshuaian would know this phrase.

"How do you know that saying?"

"Because my aunt and uncle taught it to me. Do you know Rabbi Mishi and Rabbi Yael?"

The man stood motionless for a few seconds before speaking. "Is this some sort of trick? Have you been sent here by Roman subversives to deceive us?"

"Do you know my parents?" Caleb asked. "Have you been to Tamar?"

"I do know your parents, and I have been to Tamar! I cannot believe this!" He gestured for them to enter. "Come in! Come in! Bless you!" he said. "I worked all of last night and again much of today, but I will not work these next few days. We have a calling tonight for our gathering, and I must rest before it. However, I have to show you in and welcome you. This is truly unprecedented."

Once they had entered, he closed and locked the doors. "When I was not much older than you, my family traveled to Judah, and we met your parents in a house outside of Jerusalem. It was there that they told us their story of meeting Luke."

"Yes," said Caleb. "That is near the place where my parents met."

"We all heard how they met in one of King David's tunnels under the city."

Eliza jumped on the opportunity to add to the story. "Yael was my aunt! She left our village in the middle of my mother and father's wedding ceremony to travel to Jerusalem to atone for her sins. That is when she found that tunnel!" she added with a near squeal. She hoped she was contributing to the conversation.

"You look like your aunt," said the rabbi. He decided it was time to formally introduce himself. "My name is John, and I am a student of the late Paul. He was our teacher here in the city until he was killed. He spent many of his days in the city's prisons before he died. You must have some great stories to tell, but I must rest and leave you. Otherwise, I will not be effective this evening. You have access to my assistants while I rest, and you can eat anything you like and use any of our resources. I must go to bed before this place is filled. Darkness comes early this time of year, and everyone will want to be inside of our doors before the sun sets." With that, he excused himself, telling his assistants to do anything that was asked of them.

Eliza and Caleb began a lengthy conversation with the two assistants. Barkhi watched the back-and-forth banter but said nothing. Eliza and Caleb learned of the persecution of Yeshuaians in Rome. They learned that since Paul had been killed, all of the letters that he had written to the synagogues in Roman-occupied lands had been delivered, and many copies had been made, some of them in this very room. Many Yeshuaians were coming to Rome to offer tithes and help the Yeshuaian synagogues that had sprung up after his death.

Eliza and Caleb sat and listened as they learned that the church in Rome did not lack incoming Yeshuaians looking to help. But nearly all synagogues lacked trained Yeshuaians who were prepared to travel to all parts of the Roman Empire, ready to spread His words and tell His story. The assistants said that Yeshua's message was readily received in a Roman-occupied world. Most who came to hear about the teachings of the prisoner Paul remained to help the current Roman residents in their synagogues. Few were leaving.

"We all need missionaries," said one of the assistants. "You know, people who really know the scrolls and can teach in different languages to others all around the world. Paul said we need to make saints. That's what I heard."

Caleb and Eliza enjoyed hearing about these new Yeshuaians, but Caleb had another thing on his mind as well. "We need an audience with the emperor so we can get help freeing her parents," he said.

"Just an audience?" the assistant laughed. "How old are you? Do you realize that the act of approaching the emperor incorrectly is grounds for death?"

"Well, speaking to the emperor is what we intend to do. I just need some help getting an audience. And I think I have something that will help." He pulled out his uncle's ring and put it on his middle finger. He turned it upward, so the words of Rufus's rank and the carvings on its face were visible to all. "This belonged to my uncle," he said.

Both assistants froze, looking at each other. "Well, that will be a good start. Since you want to talk to him, here is what I recommend."

For the next few minutes, the two assistants helped create a plan to get Caleb and Eliza inside the Colosseum for tomorrow's fights, where they were sure the emperor would also be.

Soon, others began arriving at the church. The first to arrive was a group of women carrying fresh food. There were many loaves of fresh bread, warm meats, vegetables, spices, and aromatic sauces. The women approached the assistants and handed them their purse. "Here is the change," said the eldest one. Without awaiting a response, she continued past everyone and walked directly to the kitchen, her other arm full of greens.

"I am going to the kitchen. I am going to get their opinion on this idea," Eliza said. She left to walk to the room where all the women went, assuming it was the kitchen area. As she went, she turned back to Caleb and spoke in Hebrew, using a dialect from Correae that she knew only he would understand. "Do not be a donkey, but do not be a carrot either."

That meant do not open your mouth and say things that you may regret, but do not close your eyes and ears and not observe all that is going on around you. Eliza wanted him to exercise discretion to protect the secrets that were worth protecting. His mother hated secrets, and her disdain for them caused her to sin and nearly die on more than one occasion.

After Eliza left, the assistants went to prepare other things, and Caleb watched the main room of the synagogue fill to capacity. Unlike the sanctuaries of the synagogues back in Judah, this one was filled with both tables and chairs. Caleb quickly figured out that this sect of Yeshuaians ate food in the same room where they worshiped and preached. In addition to the kinds of Jews Caleb was used to seeing at synagogue, there were also many homeless men and women, as well as several afflicted attendees. One group caught his attention more than the others. There was a group of three men, all of whom were blind, and they walked directly to a spot familiar to them, away from all the regular traffic. Then, to Caleb's great surprise, Rabbi John reappeared after his nap and hugged these blind men. He called Caleb over. Caleb was scared, and he walked cautiously towards the three blind men and the rabbi. He had never spoken to a blind man before.

"Yes, Rabbi John," Caleb said, with a tone of reverence.

"I want you to meet these men. I call them the three brothers, even though they are not related by blood. They all come from Gaelic parts of the empire. I just told them that the son of one of the great teachers of the Messiah has come to join us this evening, and they wanted to touch you."

"Touch me?" Caleb was not used to being touched by any man at the first meeting, let alone by a blind man, but it made sense, as these men couldn't meet him in the traditional sense.

"Come here, boy," one of the men said.

Caleb did as they instructed, and the men began asking him a series of questions as they ran their hands over him. As they explored his physique, they spoke frequently and often complimented his size and apparent strength. They marveled at the thickness of his arms. They asked him questions about his family, his home, and his wife, though he did not have the latter. One of them told him that a man his size ought to start planning to get a wife.

"Do not you want one yet?" they asked.

Caleb felt ashamed, as he had never talked with anyone about his new awareness of girls.

"Yes, I want one," he said.

"You are big, strong, and obviously smart. You made it to Rome from Judah with only your female cousin to help. You need to tell your parents you want a wife, soon," one of them said.

Caleb felt hollow, even though they had just extended some compliments to him. In that moment, he knew that his parents would never play a role in his selection of a spouse, and he would do it the same way that some sects of gentiles do, in that the men pick the women themselves.

He wondered if he really wanted a wife. He hated it when Eliza would belittle him. She seldom said nice words about his skills as a hunter, tracker, and combatant. He found that he liked the blind men's company a lot.

"Are you to be a gladiator?" one of them asked.

He chuckled before answering. "I do not think so. I want to see the emperor and get his help finding my cousin's parents. That is why we are here."

"The emperor? Oh my."

"We all have a path that we set out on. His is to speak with Titus and not be killed," said the rabbi, now rested and more talkative. However, his tone changed.

"We all have a path set by God, ordained specifically for us. You, young Caleb, are on your own path, not familiar to any of us. Most of us come looking for relief from Roman oppression. You come looking for Roman authority to assist you. I am here to tell you that the authority you seek can only come from the Messiah."

Caleb interrupted him, "Your assistants have helped me with an idea that may get us an audience with the emperor.

I do not see how the Messiah will show me where my family was taken to, nor do I know how to get that information using only prayer. I need some help, and asking the help of the emperor is the best idea we have come up with so far."

"I am not here to offer you ideas. I imagine you have heard many ideas from others smarter and wiser than I will ever be. I just do not see your encounter with the emperor resulting in an outcome that returns your aunt and uncle to you," the rabbi ended. Caleb did not want to hear that.

Caleb was respectful. He did not argue with the rabbi. However, he did choose the route of carrot, as his cousin had specifically advised against it. He shut down the conversation with a bow and decided to walk outside for some air.

It took a while to step against the flow of traffic coming into the synagogue, but he eventually made his way out into the early evening. This rabbi was not going to be of any help to them. Yet, Caleb could not deny that his assistants had some great ideas.

He was amazed to see the two assistants standing outside with him near a group of four exquisitely dressed Roman soldiers. He watched as one of the assistants handed the change purse to the men, and they put their hand on his shoulder, bowing their heads as they departed. Caleb walked to the other side of the street to stand and observe. He asked them what they were doing.

"Those men protect us from Roman aristocrats who see us as a threat and seek to harm us," explained one of the assistants. "Those soldiers are also our members, and they need that money to bribe others to turn the other cheek. Did you know that there are literally a hundred gatherings across the city just like ours every evening? And there are lots of soldiers just like those guys."

Caleb realized that he had misjudged them. He set aside his tendency to be either a donkey or a carrot. "I cannot believe it! You are using member tithes to pay bribes to protect your existence. I have never seen that. Is that okay to do?"

"We are unable to find any words of the Messiah that call self-preservation bad. In fact, our rabbi says that Yeshua Himself said, 'Give to Caesar what is Caesar's and give to God what is God's.' That coin doesn't have God's picture on it." He said, and they all laughed.

"Let's go inside. First food, then a message, then off to sleep. Do all of them together, and that is good living, yes?" Caleb rhetorically asked. Everyone smiled, nodded, and agreed. They headed to the doors to join everyone else inside.

VENGEANCE IS THE LORD'S

Caleb sat at a table with the two assistants, and they enjoyed a wonderful meal. All through the meal, the two assistants talked about what they thought would be a reasonable plan to see the emperor. They couldn't make any promises that Caleb would get to speak to or meet the emperor, but everyone agreed that they needed to see him before Caleb could meet him. Caleb suggested that they talked again when Eliza was present since her role in this plan would require a lot of coins. The assistants said that they would escort them to their room after the worship ceremony and talk through their plan as a group.

Once the meal was over, everyone moved the tables to the sides of the room, and the chairs were rearranged facing the kitchen, as this setup seemed best to accommodate everyone. Eliza and Caleb were guests of honor, and they sat together near the end of a row of chairs, with space on the right side of them for people to walk. Many people stood, as there were not enough chairs for everyone.

John told everyone that the worship service would start in a moment as the women in the kitchen first needed to finish cleaning up. Eliza returned from her time in the kitchen, and Caleb shared with Eliza that they had a new plan to get an audience with the emperor and that the two assistants would come to their room after dinner to explain it to her. She added that the women had come up with a plan, as well, and she would ask to see if two of them would also join them afterward to discuss it.

Caleb also told her about his encounter with the blind men. He made a point to mention that he liked how they sincerely complimented him, saying that he did not get that from anyone else. Eliza paused when Caleb said this. It made her feel a bit sad she was not providing for her cousin the affirmation he needed. She kept reminding herself that his parents were dead, and she was his family now. She needed to do this for him.

For her part, Eliza shared that the women in the kitchen cooked all the food not just for those who were here but also to serve the men in the city prisons. They made tasty food with excellent spices, and they would take the leftovers the following morning to the prisons, sharing them first with the guards and then with the inmates, relaying messages between synagogue leadership and those in jail. Eliza wondered if her aunt spoke to Paul while she was doing this sort of thing. She never asked the women in the kitchen if they knew Yael or if they had met Paul, but she wished she had.

Finally, the last of the women left the kitchen, signaling to John that he could start. The rabbi stood behind a small podium near the entrance to the kitchen so that everyone could see him. Everyone sang a familiar worship song; then John began to share the day's message.

"Here is a message we received just today from our friend Timothy who remains in prison," he said, after taking out a folded piece of parchment from his tunic. "I thank the Lord every day for your gifts of food. The guards treat me and my cellmates well because of your love. Although we do not always get to send you messages, we look forward to the day when we are released and can come worship with you. If that day does not come, we are looking forward to the day when we will see you at the hands of Yahweh in heaven, who has saved a seat for all who have written His name on their hearts and souls. That is the name of Yeshua."

Many in the crowd spoke up, saying, "It is so!" and "Praise the Messiah!" More than once, the crowd would interrupt John with applause. Neither Eliza nor Caleb had seen this sort of audience participation in a synagogue before, but they both liked it. It was obvious that this evening would not be boring.

The rabbi read the rest of the note. "Several days ago, we found a knife included in our food. We do not know who gave it to us. One in our group who has since sought repentance suggested that we use it to kill the guards and escape from prison. However, we were reminded of the teachings of Luke, who says, 'Vengeance is mine, says the Lord.' We knew that this knife was not a means for us to get to the outside world but instead was a trap to lure us into taking vengeance against our captors. Instead, we called over the guards and gave the knife to them, praying for our group's safety during the exchange. None of us were beaten that day, and two of the guards stayed with us, praising the Lord until the late evening. Praise God that we were able to use this temptation as a path to true freedom."

Everyone applauded again, but this part of the story made Caleb feel alone. The discussion of passing on vengeful opportunities reminded him of the choices he made both in Tamar and on the first boat to kill to protect. This cut to the core of Caleb's identity and his biggest struggle from his haunted past.

Caleb felt that he sought vengeance when his parents were killed by his systematic killing of the Roman soldiers, and he administered justice independent of any law but his own. No matter how many times Eliza told him that he had done the right thing to protect her parents, he did not believe her. Caleb learned in the house of healing that killing the perpetrators did not take away his pain. He sought relief from his pain, and that act of retribution seemed like the next right thing to do, but it did not create the desired outcome. He remained alone, without parents, while the pain of their loss lingered.

He already admitted to himself that sparing Balbi's life was both against his better judgment and the right thing to do. Now, the man who should have died has a relationship with Yeshua and a place in eternity. How is that even possible? Had he used the same judgment on Balbi that he did in Tamar, Balbi would since be dead, never having heard the story of Yeshua. That, too, would have been a crime.

"Jehovah Jireh, what is it that I am? How could you have allowed me to nurture all these skills and not use them?" he prayed under his breath. His prayers were answered.

"Young master, I wanted to say that I am grateful, um, I guess eternally grateful, for you sparing my life last week. What I did was shameful, and I do not know how you have kept me from feeling the bite of your blade or your bow," said Balbi.

Caleb had no idea that the man was next to him. Indeed, he told Balbi to meet them at the yellow door, but he did not t recall him entering. Yet, there he was.

Caleb smiled and spoke without thinking.

"I do not know either. But I am glad that I did not kill you," he said. "I am glad you are here, actually."

Caleb laughed under his breath. He had heard both of his parents talk about how funny God's methods can be. This must be one of those moments that they talked about.

Eliza greeted Balbi and spoke to Caleb during a quick intermission.

"I remember Aunt Yael just telling us that story when Luke gave her those words to write! Remember that?"

"Yes, I do," Caleb said as tears began to roll down his eyes. Eliza did not see him cry, and he was not about to let her. She might make fun of him.

Eliza did not want to include the rest of the story out loud, as they had only recently been told the entire truth. The morning that Yael figured out that she was pregnant, she felt a sense of rage and wanted to kill the Roman soldier who raped her. That day, she wrote out that verse John just mentioned when she was working for Rabbi Luke, and she confided in him that she was with child. Luke had them stop their work, and he took her for a walk. They reached the Temple grounds, and they prayed about her rape and her pregnancy at the place of destruction. Luke told her that in the same sense Yahweh could use the destruction of the Temple for good, Yeshua could use her rape for good. Uncle Rufus had escorted them there, and he told her that even if she did find and kill the man, she would have to make peace with her past. She came back and told Mishi the entire story as well, and that was the first time he told her that he loved her. There was a funny ending to the story, and Eliza jumped right to it.

"Remember when she said that your dad helped cook dinner that night for everyone, and it was awful?"

"I remember that part of the story too!" Caleb said, laughing to cover his tears.

Eliza saw through his cover this time. She reached over and touched him on the face. "You are a good man, Caleb. God has His hand on your heart. He is working great things in you. You are the proof that God can make great things and that anything is possible. You know that, right? You are most dear to me."

She needed to take care of this man. They were far from home and undertaking a risk that might kill both of them. Neither of them had completed schooling, let alone married and had children. Caleb remained unsettled, and Eliza was scared for him.

"My parents are dead, Eliza. Even after hearing that message, I would still kill the men who killed them all over again. I want to kill the men who killed Uncle Rufus, too. What am I supposed to do?"

"I do not know," she said, and they both stopped talking.

Both of them returned their focus to the rabbi as he approached the end of the evening's message. "Tomorrow, there will be a parade before the events in the Colosseum. When the emperor and his entourage walk past us, please do not openly show your disdain. Instead, pray for the man and his salvation. He does not need to be stabbed with a knife for things to be made right. We need to pray for our leaders. Yes, this man has ordered the death of many of our people. But we must not give up on him, in the same way that Yeshua did not give up on us when our ancestors killed Him during His last days in Jerusalem."

The crowd began to chant, and many of the members held hands. "Jehovah Jireh, come into the heart and soul of this man who has become the emperor and free him of the bondage that comes with his role. Bring him to You!"

"And Yeshua, let me play my part with this emperor," Eliza said. "All I want is my parents back."

As the night activities came to an end, the assistants took Eliza and Caleb to the upper room, and they settled in for the evening. Both of the assistants and two of the women joined them. The assistants began outlining their plan. To everyone's amazement, both of the women began nodding their heads.

"That is exactly what we thought these two should do, as well," they said.

For the next few minutes, the four locals began suggesting names of people that they would need help from, as well as which shops they needed to visit first thing in the morning. They explained it all to Eliza and Caleb, and they politely agreed with each action of the plan. The conversation did not take much time, and the four left, leaving Caleb and Eliza alone in the upper room.

"Good night, you two. Get some sleep. Tomorrow will be a very busy day for you!" said the oldest woman, and they departed from the view.

Caleb and Eliza took the pile of blankets and laid all of them out on the floor. They gathered on top of them and just looked at each other.

"That is simply amazing: they all came up with the same plan, independent of each other. I am feeling really good about it. Do you think you can act like they told you to?" Eliza asked.

"Sure can. I need only copy how Uncle Rufus acted when he traveled with Mom and Dad. Shouldn't be too hard," he said.

"Well, I do not know if I can pull it off," Eliza said, lacking any sense of confidence.

"Sure you can! You want to practice?" asked Caleb.

For the next few moments, the two of them sat on top of the blankets, practicing their personas. Once Eliza felt a bit more comfortable, they crawled under the blankets and blew out the last lit candle.

Caleb whispered one last thing to Eliza. "Tomorrow will be a very interesting day, cousin. I cannot wait."

"Me too," Eliza agreed, and they both fell asleep.

ENTRANCE TO THE COLOSSEUM

Long before the parade started, Caleb and Eliza awakened to begin what both knew would be an expensive day. Eliza's first stop was a hairdresser of the highest class who would charge extra coins for a same-day appointment. Since it was Colosseum day, many other women of the aristocracy were also seeking grooming, and that demand for services forced Eliza to pay ten times what it would otherwise have cost. She mentally dismissed the cost as profits from the cinnamon sales. The women from last night introduced her to a hairdresser and a seamstress, promising to bring her back looking like a Roman citizen of great nobility. After the hairdresser, they walked directly to the seamstress for house Caesar. She was talkative and loved working on someone new and with darker features than most of the paler Roman women. One of the older women brought her a few pairs of new sandals to try before she selected the ones made of black leather. With all the apparel complete, she went to the local baths for cleansing and an application of oils and perfumes. When she looked in the mirror once she was done, her breathing froze as the person looking back at her was stunning and beautiful.

"Not quite like Cleopatra, but pretty close," said the woman who held up the mirror.

In the meantime, the two assistants took Caleb to a large market filled with unique goods used exclusively by Roman soldiers, gladiators, and their women. Had Caleb know of this place yesterday, he would already have visited every one of the shops. There were also butchers in the area, as well as several blacksmiths. He speculated that these men specialized in creating weapons for the gladiators as well as providing red meat to heighten their senses during battle. There were many stalls filled with fabrics from all over the world, and many women walked openly in the city, mostly with other women and their slaves, visiting these locations and engaging shopkeepers as if they were long-lost friends. Shopkeepers routinely offered wine to the women, even though it was the middle of the day, promising them great deals if they purchased an entire bolt of cloth before the end of the day.

It was for men like him that this open-air market was created. There were several blacksmiths displaying exquisite hand-made armor and weapons beyond what anyone might ever need on an actual battlefield. There were helms, bracers, gauntlets, greaves, and plate armor fit to fight off an elephant. However, after Balbi's description of what the day's activities might look like, Caleb selected a compromise of showy and comfortable protective wear for their trek into the famous structure. Caleb purchased the lightest weight mail he could find that would fit under a robe. He then purchased a processional robe that included gold threads and double strength edges to prevent it from tearing. He bought matching greaves and bracers to protect his arms and legs. Caleb was about to spend nearly half of his money on a gold-trimmed helmet when he found a much smaller one. He liked that it wasn't red, as red was affiliated with the Roman military.

This day, the two Hebrews were on a mission to look like royalty and gain entrance through the famous blue gate where royalty from the highest of houses in the Senate and controlling merchants went. Their plan was simple: look like the Romans, then jump in the parade and walk with the Romans, then act like the Romans as you wait your turn to enter. If any problems come up, offer some coins and pray for the best.

The last and most important step for Caleb was to get a haircut and beard trimming. He also got his skin oiled and his nails cut. Once he was done, he looked as large and strong as any Roman centurion.

"How do I look?" he asked the last shopkeeper when everything was done.

"It would scare me to see you in combat," said the shopkeeper. Caleb could tell that the man had said that many times before, and it did not mean much.

"It should suffice to get you into the Colosseum," said one of the assistants.

"Good, then let's go find Eliza," Caleb replied.

They walked back to the synagogue and waited for Eliza and her entourage to return. It was early afternoon when the group of women came back, laughing like schoolgirls on the afternoon before Sabbath. Eliza was easy to spot, but she was nearly unrecognizable. All of her clothing had been replaced, the new attire made from a pure white and gold-trimmed cloth. It had purple ruffles and fine lines of woven gold thread down the center seams, making it clear that she was wealthy. Her palla cloak was full of intricate patterns that Caleb had never seen anywhere in Judah, and he was amazed at the detail. Her hair had been washed, cut, and combed and had been put up into a bun, held in place by a single silver needle worth as much as a camel. When Eliza saw Caleb, she bowed like a Roman woman might bow if the emperor himself walked past.

"You are a stupid girl!" said Caleb, but she could tell that this was not what he really thought.

"I see you like my appearance, my Lord," said Eliza in perfect Greek. "Would you escort me into the Colosseum for today's activities, my Lord?"

"Come, my Lady," said Caleb, using what they practiced last night, "This task I can do for none other than you, my princess." He spoke in perfect Greek, using only the most honorific words, just as an emperor might speak to his wife at their public wedding.

The crowd of men and women who had been helping them cheered. "You two are the most beautiful couple in all of Rome!" said one of the women who helped deliver food into the prisons. "And you look like you are most wealthy, too."

"They do not just look wealthy. They are wealthy!" Balbi chimed in. Eliza gave him her "I am mad at you" look, and everyone erupted with more laughter when the adolescent girl climbed out of the Roman princess exterior. In that moment, Balbi was correct. Had they not had the gold meant for the school on their person, they could never have afforded all this clothing and styling.

In accordance with the plan devised by the two assistants and the women, the full group of synagogue members stood and cheered as the parade approached. After the emperor and his royal entourage had passed, Caleb and Eliza joined in the parade, just as the other nobles had done when the parade passed their residences. They walked next to other couples who looked similar to them. They reached the Colosseum with the sun still high in the sky, and they did a single lap around the Colosseum, waving to the crowds before they neared the entrance. The emperor and a small group went to the left, and the rest of them were led to the right. Groups of eight Roman soldiers stopped and examined each person who approached the entrance on the right. When they reached Caleb and Eliza, Caleb put on his uncle's ring and placed the hand that wore it on his sword's hilt.

The soldier in charge looked first at Caleb, then at his ring, before asking them where they wished to sit. Caleb knew that the protocol included stating your house of membership to gain entry. "I am Caleb, nephew of the legate of the Fifth Legion, Rufus of Caesarea, son of the centurion Cornelius." He held forward his hand, showing them his uncle's ring, as the assistants instructed him to do.

"We already saw it, my Liege. You are clear to enter. Have a nice day," he said. The head soldier nodded to two others, and they, in turn, called over two escorts to lead them to their seats. Eliza gave each of them a single coin.

"Take them to sixteen beta," he said, bowing as they left his presence and entered the Colosseum.

"Come this way, my sir and my lady," said one of the two escorts. Eliza also handed each one of them a coin, bowing her head as they received them. One walked ahead of Caleb and Eliza until they reached an outdoor rampart near the center of the stadium that led to the Azure section. The other walked behind them. They passed through a simple arch in the Azure section and into their protected box. Inside were four ornately carved chairs, though they only needed two of them. Once they entered, they surveyed their home for the next hours. On the right was a large wall that separated their section from the ones used by regular citizens. They had been placed on the boundary of the royalty section. To their left were as many as a hundred boxes, each filled with people who looked just like they did.

And two boxes away on the left sat the emperor of Rome, Titus, looking for something that had not yet arrived.

Caleb's heart did not race. He only spoke a single prayer. "Thank you, Jehovah Jireh, for an opportunity to make things right for my aunt and uncle. Protect me from sin and lead us away from anxiety and needless worry. You can free them. Use this man to make that happen."

YAEL REDUX

During their superficial strut into the Colosseum, Caleb bent his non-sword arm at the elbow, allowing Eliza to place her arm through his, just as all the other couples in front of them had done. As they walked, Eliza took the time to survey the other men and women in line. She compared her cousin to the men, and she found nearly all of them lacking. Caleb was larger by all physical measures. His arms, chest, and legs were all larger and more powerful in appearance than anyone else's in the Azure line. She felt the callous on his hands and wondered if any of these men had ever actually done work. It did not matter. She was walking with royalty, and this was the grand adventure she had dreamed about. However, it was rich in betrayal of her beliefs, and she felt alone.

The women from the kitchen had let her know that she might be uncomfortable for the duration of the event. Her gown was low cut in the front, commanding the attention of the other men in line, and she observed a few of them staring further down her body. She asked the seamstress to fix the design error, but she only smiled and told her that show-ing skin was part of her admission ticket. Now that she saw the other women in line, she understood what the seamstress meant. In the common culture of the Roman Empire, all those who attended an event at the Colosseum were expected to display their body for others to see. Eliza's dress exposed more of her skin than any Hebrew ever should, and men old enough to be her father were looking at her with what she thought was ill intent. Eliza wore a necklace fashioned of perfectly hewn gems and the most detailed of gold links. Only a Hebrew jeweler could make such intricate artifacts of this quality. That, too, was the subject of attention.

Caleb's physique grabbed the attention of nearly every woman, especially all the older ones. His darker skin and defined frame caught their eye, and the smile on his face confirmed to Eliza that he liked the sexual attention. In addition, the gold that he wore was prominently placed. Caleb wore a thick bangle on his left wrist. It was of Jewish origin and one of the few items that Eliza had carried from home. Its ornate carvings were perfectly etched into the rich metal, and it was of better workmanship than anyone else's. Eliza had an eye for jewelry.

People did not only look at the two of them; many commented on how beautiful they both looked. Eliza and Caleb were unfamiliar with the unfiltered comments regarding the flesh of others, and all they knew to do was to smile, bow and extend gratitude at the perception of the compliments. During some of the moments when they were alone, they would share with each other in Hebrew that they were feeling most awkward. Eliza had never been complimented in those ways or with those words before, and Caleb could tell that she was as uncomfortable as he was.

After entering their designated boxed seats, Eliza picked up a pillow and put it in the place where she would sit today. She looked out in the Colosseum for the first time, and she felt like a Hebrew queen from the stories of old. The act of donning lavish clothing and finishing her appearance with quality Hebrew jewelry should have been enough to make this a perfect day. But it was not complete until she stood with Caleb and could see the emperor to her left. She did not look at him for long before she returned her gaze to her cousin. Caleb looked the part of a proud and seasoned warrior now. He remained her cousin, but he was now more than that. He looked like a man in every way. She was so proud of him, and she felt grateful that he was there with her.

"Thank you, my Yeshua," she whispered as she took her reserved seat inside the Colosseum. It seemed like it must be by the hand of the Messiah that she was within earshot of the most powerful person in the world. She imagined going back home and trying to tell her family and friends about this moment, but she shook her head. She remembered her aunt Yael trying to tell her cousins about her desire to explore the world outside of Correae to no avail. No one back home would understand this moment, and her story would be the stuff of fairy tales. Her smile was as much full of melancholy as it was of joy.

"You know, my dear, no one will believe us when we tell them we did this," she said to Caleb, using formal Greek but in a low tone. She knew it was possible that others could overhear their words, so she left her comment vague enough for there to be room for interpretation.

"Perhaps." Caleb copied tone and ambiguity. He knew what she meant.

The Flavian Amphitheatre, as it was called, was over four hundred cubits long, making it much larger than the Temple. At one hundred cubits high, it was taller than Noah's Ark. The Amphitheatre was referred to as one of the "seven wonders" of the world due to its grandeur. Its exterior was concrete and brick, and the concrete surfaces had been painted to hold vibrant colors. These colored facades gave the gates their names. While waiting in line to enter, they heard much small talk about how rich the painted walls looked this time of year when the sun shined upon them. It was remarkable how identical the color of the wall was to the sea.

But what filled the hearts of the Romans who could afford to enter the Colosseum was that human death was on public display for all to see. The sights and sounds that came from the center of the theatre were gruesome ones. Yet, the Romans thought them to be "grand." Orgies afterward were common, confirming her impression that this place and those who entered it were evil. Although neither Eliza nor Caleb had any intention of attending one of these orgies, they knew they needed to look the part to pass through the security checks. The Romans safeguarded their entrances for good reasons. The number of emperors assassinated in the last fifty years required more than there are fingers on both hands to count.

Although the original construction was started under Vespasian, it was not until Titus took the throne last year that the Colosseum was completed. Titus was said to have used much of the wealth he acquired during the siege on Jerusalem to finance the work. To economically justify his investment, Titus sold off the rights to certain days of the month for individuals to hold their own events at the Colosseum. Titus himself only came when he knew that gladiators would be present, but he collected royalties on all events, including the ones he did not attend.

Their seats were in boxes, so called because there was a wall of brick on all sides of them. The back wall was high enough to prevent anyone from looking into their booth from the hallways that lead them there. The walls both to the left and to the right kept patrons from seeing each other, but only if they were seated. If they stood up and went to the edge, they could see the others in the adjacent box. All pit fighting was in front of them, and nothing was placed there that might impede their vision or experience.

Screened and vetted food vendors started coming through their booth as they saw it occupied. They had a large variety of freshly prepared food to offer as well as many wines to choose from. Both Caleb and Eliza politely declined all food and beverages, and they used the encounters with the vendors to ask a lot of questions about the day's events. All that remained was the small matter of getting an audience with the emperor, who sat two boxes to the left.

As Eliza and Caleb spoke to each other, they noticed that a slightly older girl dressed in all white adorned with gold had entered their box and stood near them without speaking. Caleb had seen an identical girl in the emperor's box and wondered if she was the same person. She did not appear to be selling anything. Caleb motioned for her to come to them.

"Good afternoon," she said. "I have been assigned to assist you during the time at Colosseum. Tell me what you need, and I will do it to you." She had a slight accent and poor Greek grammar. She was obviously not a native Greek speaker.

"So, what events have transpired that relocated you to Rome as an indentured servant?" Eliza asked in perfect Hebrew. She made sure to use larger nouns and verbs to confirm that she knew real Hebrew, not the street version often spoken by Romans who tried to sell to Jews.

"Ma'am, I do not..." the girl started.

"What is your name?" Eliza interrupted. "Your Hebrew name!"

Caleb followed up her demanding question with some of his own. "You understand us, yes? So, what is your name?" Caleb spoke in a gentle voice, though. He and Eliza had much practice speaking to strangers in alternating tones to get information from them.

"Yael," the girl said in perfect Hebrew. "My name is Yael. Yael is a Hebrew name."

Caleb had just placed a small piece of fresh bread and hummus in his mouth when she spoke. His jaw dropped, and some food fell out as she said her name the second time. He quickly apologized, and the girl bent over to pick up the dropped piece of food. "You know, that was my mother's name!" Caleb said as he helped her pick up the crumbs off of the well-swept stone floor.

"In the name of the Messiah!" Yael exclaimed. "When I attended school, one of our traveling rabbis was a woman whose name was also Yael! I was told that she was the only female rabbi in all of Judea." Yael covered her mouth to stifle a shriek. She had just referred to Judah in the original Hebrew form, Judea, and she quickly remembered that Judea was a forbidden word.

This loud conversation in a foreign tongue brought the attention of the Roman couple in the luxury booth next to theirs, and they peered over the edge to see what the source of the commotion was.

"Please excuse us," Caleb said politely. "We got lost in a story. Please enjoy your afternoon," said Caleb, using perfect and polite Greek. The middle-aged couple stepped back from the brick barricade and returned to their seats, no longer to be seen. Yael smiled, stepped outside, and hung a "do not disturb" sign above their archway, thereby shutting off vendor visits. She and Eliza giggled for a moment, both of them feeling a natural ease with each other that could not have been scripted. Eliza quickly told her how much she hated the clothing that she was wearing, feeling that she was all but exposed for everyone to see her. Yael quickly agreed, wishing for a quality cloak from Judah that she could wear to keep warm when it was windy. Within moments, they were complaining about the taste of some Roman food but also marveling at how much they enjoyed all the selections in the market. It was as if they had known each other for years.

The parade began on the Colosseum's main floor. The first to enter were flag bearers and trumpeters. The crowd cheered, and many of the royalty near them called out the names of the gladiators that they had sponsored and had come out to see fight. This distraction gave the newly acquainted friends a chance to interact freely with no concern of eavesdropping.

They experienced a rare moment when they all got to be Jewish children again, leaving behind the burdens that enslavement and foreign occupation created. Caleb picked on the girls as if they were all in school, and the girls found joy in asking him questions that he could not answer. They talked until the parade was nearly over, and all three of them felt safe, despite the nearby presence of the enemy of their people.

Caleb was impressed with how much of his mother's teaching this girl knew. He asked her lots of questions, and in return, she provided them with great intelligence about Rome. For her part, Yael worked at one of the houses of Caesar and was "leased" out to the Colosseum management company on a per-event basis. Today, she was sent to this box by her supervisors, but she had tomorrow off from work.

She also told them of the many Yeshuaian synagogues all over the city, and many of their members were current and former Roman military. A lot of the converts had come to know the Messiah from the remarkable tales related to the prisoner Paul. The city was experiencing a mass awakening of faith, and people were migrating away from their polytheistic roots to Yeshua. It was rare, indeed, to find a Yeshuaian synagogue that did not have the Roman military and Roman prison guards as members. Caleb recounted his story of seeing Roman soldiers outside the church with the yellow door, and Yael nodded, assuring him that this was normal now.

Yael did not paint a perfect world for Yeshuaians in Rome. Most people were not sympathetic to their cause. Most Yeshuaians faced physical danger, as Roman citizens, guards, and soldiers considered faith in any god other than the emperor to be unlawful. They did not speak out against the emperor in public, as this act often ended in martyrdom. Nearly all the local Yeshuaian rabbis taught them to follow Yeshua in all things but not to foolishly cast their life away to make their point. Instead, they were taught to engage in prayer for those who did not know the Messiah as they went about their days in the capital city.

Yael told them that since Titus had become emperor, there had been no edicts that restricted Yeshuaians, as there had been under emperor Vespasian or those from the line of Caesar who came before him; but the old edicts remained. Although outside gatherings in public were not allowed, there were few barriers to having private events or Sabbath gatherings that included traditional Hebrew customs. Members of the Senate disagreed, but Titus would often remind them of their obligation to serve the people, and few defied him.

"This new emperor has been a great blessing to us. This emperor does not see the Messiah as the threat as those who have come before him," Yael said.

"My uncle Rufus taught me nearly all I know about hunting and combat," Caleb said. "He was best friends with Titus when the two of them entered the Roman military. They traveled the world together, conquering lands and peoples in Britannia, Gaul, and our native Judea. Once Rufus saw that a life without belief in the Messiah was meaningless, he quit the military at the rank of the legate, and he stayed back in Judah. He married a Hebrew girl, and he served as a protector for the remaining synagogues that were near Jerusalem. He did not have any children of his own, though. I guess I was his child," said Caleb, speaking out loud words that he had never thought.

"That is incredible. May Jehovah Jireh extend His grace and give her children."

"He was killed a few weeks ago. I have his ring." Caleb held up his left hand, showing her the intricate metal and gemstone artifact on his middle finger.

"I do not know what to say," she replied. "God has a purpose for you being here this very day. You know, I feel like I am watching history being made."

Yael continued talking about what the emperor had done in the last few weeks. Titus had extended freedom of worship to the polytheistic Greeks and sun god-worshipping Egyptians who had been brought into the city to help with the rebuilding after the fire. Rome was a melting pot of culture and religion these days. Titus saw much value in his vision for a more architectural Rome built for the residents of all Roman lands. He wanted them to have a sense of ownership in the city and its culture. Titus chose to extend a Sabbath grace not just to the Jews but to all faiths that had their own equivalent of a day of rest.

"Get this! The emperor has lots of sexual relations but currently lives with only one concubine, and she is Hebrew! On the weekends or when he is away, I serve her."

"Really?" said Caleb. He wanted some evidence that his uncle's descriptions of the emperor were true. "Does he really have excellent aim with a javelin, even at fifty cubits?" he asked. Yael stared at him like he was from the top of Mount Ararat. She had no idea how to respond.

"I see him eat, have sex, hear complaints, and issue edicts. I have never seen him in a combat situation."

This did not deter Caleb's effort to talk about combat and hunting. He repeated tales that his uncle Rufus had told him about his best friend before he had become emperor. He told her how Rufus' father was the famous centurion spoken of in the new writings of their faith. The girls politely listened, but they did not care.

"Both his parents and mine watched Cornelius the centurion baptize Rufus in my hometown," said Eliza proudly. Titus was invited to that event, but he did not come.

"Titus has heard of the Messiah from Uncle Rufus," Caleb explained. "Uncle Rufus left Titus after the fall of Jerusalem, but the two of them saw each other many times after that," said Caleb, as he continued to recount some stories.

Rufus had told Caleb of Titus' womanizing and how he would pick out women in the opposing people's villages who he would bed immediately after defeating them. Titus did not select gold as his primary spoils of war. He collected unique females to mate with. Nor did Rufus prioritize gold as his item of greatest interest from the spoils of war. Instead, he collected artifacts and relics from each culture that they conquered. After Rufus became a Yeshuaian and began contributing to the synagogue, he donated those items that he took from the Temple after its collapse. This included the scrolls of Jesus' brother James.

Eliza's brain raced. She felt a call upon her soul that must have been the Holy Spirit. It was the same one that came when she had forgiven Balbi. She breathed deeply, then exhaled. Puzzled, the others looked at her, but they had no idea what was happening.

"Do you think you could arrange a chance meeting for us with Titus or his concubine?" she asked. Before allowing Yael the chance to answer, Eliza told her the complete story of her parents being captured and their need to get help from the emperor.

Yael stared straight ahead in disbelief at what she had just been asked. She then nodded and spoke.

"Hmm. I think so. The emperor is relatively approachable. I have an idea that should work. Stand by the arches and look for me to signal you. When I do, come immediately. Once I point you towards the emperor, he will probably be alone. You will be on your own after that. However, I will continue to pray for you without ceasing. You must do the same. Agreed?"

Even though Eliza said, "yes!" and jumped up and down, Yael looked only at Caleb and pointed at him, saying, "That was a teaching I learned from your mother!"

Eliza looked to the sky, forgetting where she was, raising her hands to the heavens and speaking out to God, just as she had seen her aunt Yael do countless times. "Living God, Jehovah Jireh, may Your will come to be. Allow me to be a servant and use this man to bring my family back together. I ask these things in Your Son's name. Amen."

A Meeting at the Emperor's Throne

Eliza stood by the archway leading into their booth while Caleb watched the proceedings in the pits below them with great interest. Eliza was on the lookout for a sign from Yael that it was time to meet the emperor. All the while, she prayed.

Caleb had absorbed everything that Yael had told him about the goings-on inside the Colosseum. Apparently, every event was sponsored either by a specific person or the empire. *Munera* were paid for, in advance, by wealthy families, and those who purchased the rights to hold these events would sell admission or allow entrance at no cost to earn the adoration of the Roman citizens who attended. Rome, acting as a nation/state, would hold events called *ludi* for citizens as spectacles to display justice and its associated bloodshed. These included great acts of punishment, maiming, and death. The Roman Senate concluded that these events, when they were public and well-marketed, gave both citizens and slaves something to talk about other than the dullness of their daily lives. The Colosseum provided meaning for what might otherwise be a meaningless life. In addition, during *ludi*, individuals accused of crimes would be fed to wild animals or be forced to fight newer gladiators to give the newer fighters some much-needed experience. This reinforced the consequences of breaking the law, keeping the city fearful of defiance.

During both *munera* and *ludi*, the main attraction was the fights that pitted one house's gladiator against another house's gladiator. The outcomes of these battles brought great glory to the winner and death to the loser. Many of the gladiators carried the signa of their sponsoring house on their helmets and armor as advertising for their family and the family's business. Once their gladiator entered combat, a representative from each house would be escorted to the pits below where they could step out at the conclusion of the battle to celebrate the victory with their gladiator. For the royalty in attendance, the possibility of being present during the celebration made the act of going to the Colosseum worth the cost of investing in a gladiator sponsorship. For the wealthy, supporting a gladiator meant living a life of glory without the risk of dying in battle.

Caleb watched two events from beginning to end while they waited for a sign from Yael. During the first one, a younger man who had been found guilty of stealing from a market vendor on two different occasions had to fight a beast. His penalty was to combat a pack of hungry dogs. He was set free to run on the sand-covered pits while the dogs chased him. Prior to the *ludi*, the dogs were denied any food for three days. A number that the handlers had determined meant they would be the most aggressive yet still strong enough to overcome him if he fought back. The boy was given only a knife.

The boy looked up at the emperor, crying out for mercy, as he climbed on blocks of marble placed strategically in the pits for combatants to use as protection. Occasionally, a man on a horse would come out with a whip. He would strike the boy, making him move off the block he was standing on and run for his life to another block while the dogs chased him. It only took two whippings before one of the dogs caught the boy by an ankle, and they began tearing into his pinned leg. He kicked in resistance, trying to stab at them, but he never wounded any of them. Eventually, a larger male dog sunk its teeth into his other leg, biting through a nerve and leaving the boy immobilized. Caleb thought that the dogs would attempt to sever the arteries in the neck, as they would do with a deer, but they did not. The sound of the boy as he was eaten alive caused many of the men in the royalty section to laugh. Caleb could not laugh; he was disgusted at the justice served in this place. His cousin covered her ears, obviously still praying, and Caleb decided to pray as well. That boy was nearly his age and was inadequately prepared to defend himself. Caleb found the hearts of the men who orchestrated this event detestable. He thought the fight was unfair, but he did dare not speak up. He had learned from his attempts at retaliation in Tamar that vengeance was not his to administer, so he spoke only to himself under his breath. "Vengeance is God's to administer. Lord, you have to solve this one."

As the boy cried out and could no longer resist the starved animals, Caleb recalled one of his father's teachings. "There will come a day when we breathe no more, and we will stand in front of the Messiah, the Father, and the Holy Spirit. We will account for our actions. Those who do not have the Messiah will be found guilty of sin, and they will pay a penalty for that sin that makes the worst abomination on earth seem trivial."

And it will be worse than this? Caleb thought.

Once the match was over, three young Egyptian women carrying baskets on their heads came out and picked up the remains of the boy, placing the entrails in their baskets before returning to the caves under the pits. The man on the horse climbed down, calling over the dogs and petting two of them before leading them through a portcullis and down into the dungeons below. The dogs had been fed, and it was time to put them away.

Caleb could not believe that that boy's life had been given such low value. He imagined that the contents of those baskets would become a meal for another animal in residence below the pits. He prayed again. "Jehovah Jireh, may that boy's soul be with You now, just as my parents are. This boy did not deserve this grisly end. Let him find peace with You."

Without an intermission, the second event started. This match began with lengthy introductions that were interrupted by the crowd with cheers. A single gladiator from one of the houses of Caesar was introduced, and he wore great armor and a gold-covered helmet. On the other side, a tall and powerful-looking Egyptian was introduced, who was called the "modern Goliath" to the crowd by the crier. The Egyptian towered over everyone else and wore only a helmet and chest covering of leather hide. He carried out three javelins and three spears which were like ones the Roman military carried but much longer and tipped with what appeared to be a polished form of wrought iron. He set out placing them in strategic places around the pit as he raised his fists, bringing down floods of applause. The other gladiator carried only a single gladius and small shield of the sort that made gladiators famous.

The emperor and everyone else stood up and stopped talking. He raised his hand and spoke. "You shall fight to the death or until I tell you to stop. Do you understand the penalty of disobedience?" Both men looked up and him and nodded.

"Begin," he said coolly. The crowd erupted with noise, and men yelled down to the pits their recommendations for combat. Caleb could tell that there was a split in loyalties between the Egyptian and the Roman. Everyone in his section rooted for one of the two men, but Caleb could not see any patterns.

The gladiator charged first, holding his weapon with one hand and his small shield in the other. Caleb loved the size and shape of his weapon. He speculated on how easy it must be to use it compared to the javelin and spear combination that the Egyptian used. Success could only occur in close proximity to the swordsman.

As he charged, the soldier raised his fist to the crowd. Nearing the Egyptian, he rolled on the ground as the towering Egyptian launched a javelin at him. The Roman intentionally went to the ground and rolled twice, bringing him close enough to strike. His bade was sharp, and it connected with his opponent. Blood rapidly began to flow from the Egyptian's right leg as the blade sliced deeply. Using a spear, the Egyptian responded by attempting to pierce the fighter but failed to plunge the point into an unarmored location. The fighter rolled again to separate himself from the Egyptian. He stood back up and attempted to run behind a nearby marble block. Although the Egyptian was wounded in his leg, he was able to hurl the javelin at his combatant before he reached cover. It struck with a force hard enough to knock the man down. The Roman's back was not as well armored as his front, and Caleb speculated that the Egyptian hit his kidney. The Egyptian moved to pick up one of his spears and hobbled towards the stunned man, placing minimal weight on his injured ankle. The fighter was able to rotate to expose his more protected front side, and the spear glanced off of his armor. From the ground, the Roman swung at the man's already injured leg, hoping to destroy it. However, he had let himself get too close. The Egyptian knew his spear would not be effective against this man's armor, so he picked up the gladiator and threw him into the air, hoping that the impact and the inward folding of his armor when he hit would stun him. On his way up, the armored combatant struck the Egyptian on the shoulder, and the blade bit into his flesh. He dropped the gladiator before he could get him over his head, but the force of the armor on the man's smaller frame made him scream. The gladiator clung to his gladius, as his life depended on it.

The crowd was cheering so loudly that it was deafening, but Caleb was surprised to see that the Emperor was not cheering. The Egyptian picked the man up a second time, and this time the gladiator struck the Egyptian's forearm. The blow was not strong, but his blade was sharp, and the Egyptian was unarmored. Blood immediately poured from this new wound. Again, the Egyptian dropped the man and covered the wound with his hand to stop the bleeding, screaming with rage. The fighter used that moment to roll away from this Goliath and attempt to stand up. He could not, as Caleb thought he had broken several ribs and lacked the strength.

Both were now seriously wounded, and the gladiator tried to hold his chest through his armor, his lungs obviously damaged as well by the impact. Men wearing armor were not meant to be thrown. The Egyptian figured this out.

Caleb gave the advantage to the Egyptian. Although he had wounds to his leg, shoulder, and forearm, he was still mobile and able to wield all of his weapons. He still had two nearby javelins in the arena to use, and one was right next to him. In his present state, there was no way that the injured gladiator could sustain his assault.

A pattern emerged. The Egyptian would throw javelins at the gladiator as he attempted to close the distance between them. Any time the fighter would attempt to close the gap, the Egyptian would thrust the javelin at the man's exposed legs, and the fighter would be forced to retreat. Eventually, one of the Egyptian's throws struck an exposed part of the gladiator's armor and pierced his chest. The fighter was now irrecoverably wounded. The Egyptian grabbed his final spear and thrust his long weapon into the exposed thigh of his opponent, sending him permanently to the ground. The Egyptian left the spear in the man's leg and walked to retrieve another as the crowd screamed for him to finish the gladiator. Since the Egyptian's ankle was now beginning to fail him, this took a great deal of time.

The crowd began to chant. Some still rooted for the gladiator to pull out the javelin and get back into the fight. However, his will to fight back was now gone, for he knew that even if he pulled out the spear, he would never be able to close the gap on the Egyptian and get close enough to strike at his flesh.

As was the custom, the gladiator threw his gladius on the ground in front of the soon-to-be winner and gave up. The Egyptian made no spectacle of the man's choice to submit, and he pushed his final spear into his neck and out the other side, spilling the man's blood onto the sand.

Many people rejoiced in the goriness of the ending. The men chatted with each other, each suggesting what the combatants could have done differently. Caleb had seen enough. He walked back to where his cousin awaited a signal from Yael. Eliza was glad to see him, as she was a bit overwhelmed by blocking out the sounds of the match while watching for a sign from Yael.

"Caleb, how you can watch that?" He knew better than to respond. She continued on with a different line of conversation, "I've been thinking. I do not think it was by chance that this Yael knew your mother. I do not think our meeting with her was a chance either. I think what we are seeing is the presence of Yahweh. God is bigger than circumstance. Our prayers are being answered, right now, in this place of evil!"

"Maybe. That first boy's prayers weren't being answered," Caleb replied.

"I've been watching the emperor, too. During the last battle, he seemed distracted. He did not talk to anyone, even his attendant girls, and I think he's lonely. He did not drink any wine or eat. After watching how he did not care about that ending, I do not know what I think about him. Something is missing from his life. Uncle Rufus talked to me about why he quit the military. He said that no matter how successful he was in the eyes of Rome, it never fulfilled him. The emperor hasn't seen yet that he is the same as Uncle Rufus in that regard."

"Wait, Yael is signaling us!" Eliza interrupted. "Come on!"

Both of them immediately left their box and headed towards Yael. Caleb walked on the left side of Eliza, as was customary among Roman royalty, and she stepped slightly behind him, extending reverence to him as her leader.

Yael gestured for them to hurry. She stood near an arch that led to the bathroom. "The emperor just entered the bathroom during the intermission! If you want an audience with him, go find him in there."

Caleb nodded and entered the bathroom. He rounded the corner, and there sat Titus, his royal robe hanging on a hook built into the wall next to his toilet. Caleb looked directly at him and addressed him in a confident voice. "I am

Rufus's nephew, and I am from Judea," he began. He knew that it was the emperor's order that the entire land now be called "Judah," but he also knew that Titus had been there when it was called "Judea." He risked offending the emperor in doing this but challenging him seemed like the quickest way to earn his respect. Titus looked intrigued. "My family needs your help," he continued. Next came the most difficult part. He needed to be quiet and wait for the emperor to respond.

"And you have some proof that you are his nephew, I assume?" Titus asked.

Caleb had expected this, and he had practiced his response with Eliza on the boat ride over here. He took off his uncle Rufus's ring and casually tossed it to the emperor.

Titus caught it and inspected it. "Incredible," he said. "I remember when he got this ring."

"My uncle said that when you were boys, you would run outside on the Palatine Hill, and the first one to the top of the hill would throw stones at the other while they finished. He said you would always catch the stones when he beat you. That is why I threw it to you instead of handing it to you."

"Is that so?" said Titus, cracking a smile. "Oh, Rufus. I do miss him." It was apparent that emperor Titus, ruler of the Roman Empire and all its lands, was still a boy at heart. Caleb and Eliza's strategy to bring him back to the old memories that he kept of Rufus had succeeded. "So, did Rufus give you this ring, or did you steal it from him? And what is it that you need?"

"It is not for me that I am here. It is for my family," Caleb said. He turned his head back towards the entrance and called out. "Eliza! Come in here, please."

Although he was done with his ablutions, Titus remained seated as Eliza entered. Yael stayed outside.

"Your Highness," said Eliza as she entered. She acted like a Roman woman might act when coming into the presence of the emperor, bowing down and not making eye contact with him.

"So, you are also Hebrew, yet you look and act like a Roman woman of wealth," Titus said, and Eliza caught a glimmer of admiration in his tone.

"Well done with your disguise, little one." He used the Hebrew term of affection. She knew this man to be fond of flesh, and Eliza immediately got scared.

Titus stood up, washed himself with a water challis, and donned his royal robe again. He walked towards the exit, holding the ring, gesturing for Eliza and Caleb to follow. Yael was at the exit, with her head bowed as the three of them walked out. Once they cleared that area, he turned to them and spoke. "So, how is old Rufus these days?" he asked.

"My uncle is dead," Caleb said. "He was killed unarmed in Mishi and Yael's village a few weeks ago. The men who did it were current soldiers of yours."

"Do you remember Mishi?" Eliza interjected. She knew that action was the only method to consistently combat her fear. "He was the young rabbi who spent the first days with Rufus after the fall of the Temple!"

"I do. He was a skinny one, but he could talk to any of us, and he was quite funny if I remember correctly."

"He was my father," said Caleb, standing up straight. He knew that the Roman military mandated absolute reverence to the bloodline.

Titus looked the boy in the eye, then examined his body. The emperor nodded his approval of Caleb's physique, but Caleb remained a bit scared. Caleb appeared strong, but in his heart, he feared that the emperor might ask him why he did not have the physique that his father had at that age. He was not ready for that question. "What happened to those men, the ones who killed old Rufus?" Titus asked instead.

"I killed them, emperor," said Caleb.

Titus nodded. It was now apparent that the emperor respected this young boy. But Caleb no longer had a script of questions for him to follow. All that they had hoped to accomplish was to meet Titus and connect with him. They had already gotten far beyond what they had imagined.

"And how did you do that?" Titus asked. Caleb had just watched how the emperor observed the gladiator battle, and he told his story with details that he thought the emperor would appreciate. He included his response to seeing his parents take their last breath as his justification for killing the Romans. He showed him the injury to his forehead that happened right before he slit the throat of the centurion with his counter. He also explained his choice to rip through the calf muscle as deeply as he could before attempting to retreat and proactively strike. He recalled the number of steps he had taken and how he had removed his uncle's ring after Rufus had gestured to him to do so.

"Your recall of the details of such an event is impressive. You are obviously Rufus's student, yes?" he asked.

"Yes, he was my instructor," said Caleb. The emperor paused for a minute before speaking.

"So, you killed my soldiers and one of my centurions, and you come asking for permission to find this girl's parents to set them free without any consequences for your actions? Is that true?"

"Yes, I do, and yes, it is," said Caleb. "Your Highness," he added quickly.

"Well, you are a brave boy. I may give you what you seek, but it will come at a cost. Consider it a consequence for the destruction of my property."

"We're listening," said Eliza.

"She speaks with courage as well, I see, despite not being spoken to."

"Please forgive her," said Caleb. "She is a young girl who wants her parents back. I only wish to honor her and my parents." That brought a smile to the emperor's face, bigger than anything Caleb had seen during the gladiator fights.

"I will ask you for two things. If you can give me one of them, I may give you what you ask for to set your parents free."

Fear entered both of their hearts. Whatever the emperor was about to offer was going to require sacrifice. Of this, they were sure. They just did not know what he was about to ask.

THE CHOICE VERSUS THE OUTCOME

Without ever making eye contact with Caleb, the emperor spoke while adjusting his robes now that he was back from the restroom. Your first option is to fight in my pits this very day," the emperor said.

"Your Highness, I do not want to kill innocent people," Caleb replied without hesitation. His uncle Rufus taught him that in the military, it was important to respond only to the question or circumstance at hand. He wanted to say more but knew that his next step was to be courageous and wait for the emperor to offer the alternative. After all, the emperor had said that he would give Caleb two choices.

"Very well. The alternative is that I will bed these two Jewish girls, right now. The choice is yours."

With that, the emperor began a slow walk back towards his box, gesturing at Yael and Eliza to follow him. Eliza looked back at Caleb with horror as she followed behind Yael and the emperor.

In a flash, Caleb recalled a talk with his mother a few weeks ago. She had just told him that she was raped.

"My son, you are a beautiful boy, and you are becoming a beautiful man," she had said. "Many people admire your strength, but we live in a dangerous world."

"Mom, why did you not fight back? Kick him or something?"

"I was scared. I was also upset at all the things happening around me. I had just seen atrocities that no person should ever have to see. But there will come a day when we all must see what we do not wish to see and do what we do not wish to do. It is my prayer that you act when that moment is upon you and do not feel paralyzed as I did."

Caleb saw this as his moment. It was exactly what his mother was talking to him about. His choice was difficult, with either outcome resulting in people getting hurt. Should he fight and kill innocent people to save his cousin and their new friend, or should he let them be defiled in the same manner that his mother let herself be defiled?

The emperor was now only a few steps away from the archway into the royal box, and the two guards who screened all entrants in and out stood at attention to the emperor to enter. Titus paused to look back at the girls, speaking loudly enough for Caleb to hear. "Take off your robe and undergarments after you enter my booth and come to me."

Under his breath, Caleb muttered, "Yes, Mother. I will take action." He raised his voice and spoke to Titus. "I have chosen! I will not give up my sisters' virginity." Caleb yelled out to the emperor and began briskly walking towards him.

Caleb committed at the highest of levels by calling Yael and Eliza his sisters. That now meant that their honor was his honor and their dishonor was his dishonor. Yeshua expressed intimacy when he called his listeners his brothers and sisters. He called all of his disciples' brothers, not students. His parents had told him that to embrace someone as a brother or sister is to regard them as equal to yourself in all ways. Caleb needed these two people to be equal in importance for him to kill on their behalf.

He reached Yael and Eliza first, and he paused to hold their forearms. By now, the emperor had two additional soldiers with him, and he was giving the senior one orders to change the sequence of events and place Caleb fourth in line on the day's docket.

"Your sister?" said Yael, literally in disbelief at what she had just heard and the honor just bestowed. "I cannot accept this burden!" she said.

Eliza also pleaded with Caleb. "Please, just let this crazy ultimatum pass. My parents' lives are worth more than my body!"

"Caleb, I am no virgin," said Yael. "I have been bedded by royalty after events like these against my will in the past, and I can survive it. Do not give your life so foolishly for us." Caleb could see right through her strategy to sway him with guilt. It did not work, but he did respond to her. "That act that you have been required to perform for these brutes shall cease this very day," he said, taking extra effort to control his desire to emotionally erupt.

Caleb broke his grasp on the girls and walked towards the archway leading into the emperor's reserved booth. The guard let him pass.

As he was about to walk inside the emperor's box, the two girls made one last effort to dissuade him from casting aside his life for a moment like this. "Caleb, let us do this thing!" Eliza said. "We do not want you to die because of this. What you are thinking is folly! Our act will pass quickly." When Caleb failed to respond, the two girls followed him and entered the emperor's booth themselves.

"If you want a combat, I will give it to you," Caleb said firmly to Titus. "Promise me that you will leave both of my sisters alone, and I will fight to the death. Will you promise me this?"

"I am the emperor," Titus said. "I make no promises to anyone, let alone a Jew. Remember, I destroyed your Temple."

Caleb knew not to let personal assaults break his focus as a soldier. Uncle Rufus had practiced these sorts of verbal assaults with Caleb when they were walking back from their hunts. Caleb allowed the words to pass, and he focused his efforts on his cause. That was the tenant of his teachings.

"My uncle said you were an honorable man. If I kill for all to see, will you leave my Hebrew sisters undefiled?"

Caleb was not truly speaking for the girls, however. He was speaking for his mother. Caleb had decided that he would gladly give his life to prevent such an event as his mother's rape from happening to another generation of Hebrew girls.

"Take him down to the pits," the emperor said to the guards. Caleb decided that this meant yes.

Uncle Rufus gave his parents the writings he had acquired of Yeshua's brother, John. One of those writings spoke to him in this moment; it gave him peace. "There is no greater love than to lay down one's life for one's friends." The only difference was that they were now his family.

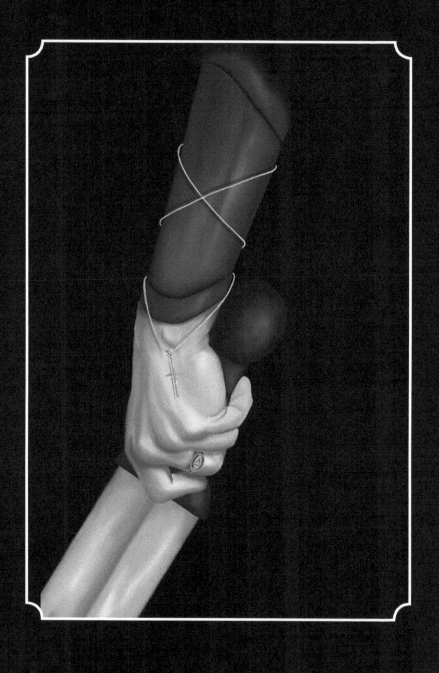

LIFE EXPANDS AND CONTRACTS

Caleb was led by one of the emperor's soldiers through a series of passageways under the Colosseum towards a pre-fight staging area. On the way, they passed an entrance gated by a portcullis that led to the fighting pits, and he could see and hear combat of the battle before his. Caleb paused to look at the two men currently fighting. One of the combatants was seasoned, fully aware that there was no urgency to end the match. The other one had a look of desperation on his face as he circled the older fighter. Both appeared to be injured. That was probably the reason for the cheering. They paused and watched for a moment before the soldier pressed for them to keep moving. As the noise reached a crescendo, Caleb wondered who had scored the big hit. Did the patience of the seasoned combatant win, or did the desperation of the younger warrior?

"Who won?" Caleb asked the soldier.

"No one yet. They aren't loud enough for there to have been a victor yet."

"I've never done this."

"What have you done then?" asked the soldier.

"I have hunted animals and killed a couple of Roman soldiers and their centurion. That's about it."

"Really? How did you kill the centurion?"

Caleb told him of the attack on his village. He told him how he used controlled cutting, rolling, and luring to get the centurion to overcommit and leave himself vulnerable. He showed his wound on his forehead, just as he had done with the emperor moments earlier.

"That is most impressive! A combatant who thinks!" said the soldier with genuine respect. They arrived at the staging area next to the entrance to the pits. Two other young boys approached Caleb and the soldier, asking them what sorts of weapons and armor they wished for.

"I need a bow and some weighted arrows. I also need two hunting knives," Caleb spoke as clearly as he could to make sure he got exactly what he was looking for. "I do not want them if they do not have a metal tip. I will keep this light armor that I am wearing," he took off his fancy robe and gave it to the boys to hang up. "I want some lighter and better-strapped sandals, though."

"What about you?" said one of the young boys.

"I'm good, Mark," said the soldier who had been escorting Caleb to the pits. He took off his cloak and handed it to the boy, who hung it on a nail near the gates. He picked up an ornate shield from a nail on the wall and unsheathed his sword, handing it to the other boy to sharpen and polish.

Caleb's heart fell as he realized that he might have been taken to the pits by the very person he would be fighting. He watched the soldier begin a stretching routine to prepare for combat. A sense of fear came over him. It was obvious that this man had many more years of fighting behind him than Caleb did and that he was on a first-name basis with the boys who assisted the gladiators. Once again, Caleb had talked too much, revealing some of his fighting strategies, and he began to feel a sense of panic.

"Am I fighting you?" Caleb asked the man in a sheepish tone. As he awaited an answer, thoughts raced through his mind. Was it too late to go back and offer his cousin's virginity in exchange? How many of Caleb's weaknesses had the soldier uncovered?

Words from his mother passed into his mind. "Do not be afraid, my son. The Messiah is always with you." Caleb felt strengthened by this. He breathed in and exhaled. He had a new peace.

"No, we are fighting together, and I needed to know something about my partner," said the soldier, laughing at how silly Caleb's question sounded.

Caleb laughed with the soldier and placed an arm on his shoulder, an act that connects two soldiers. It was another tool he had learned from his uncle. He prayed out loud. "Yeshua, You are in control," he said aloud in Hebrew. "Forgive me for not trusting You."

"What was that?" asked the soldier in Greek. It was only then that Caleb realized that the man did not recognize Hebrew from its sound.

"Nothing," Caleb responded. "I was just talking in my native language."

The other soldier turned to the two boys. "Who do we fight today?" he asked.

"There are two men who were found to be worshipping a god other than the emperor. You have probably seen them. They have fought here before," said one of them.

Caleb could not imagine the task he was about to engage in. All he envisioned were people who looked like the ones his parents would serve at their synagogue being put to death by his hands. But he also knew that he must consider them to be more like wild game to be hunted and killed. Both Eliza's and Yael's lives depended on it.

"What god?" Caleb asked. Caleb wanted them to be worshippers of the sun god so that he could justify his upcoming actions. But he knew that he must do this deed regardless of who they worshipped.

"I do not know," said Mark, as he sifted through the armory, looking for the best bow available. He found one and gave it to Caleb. Caleb took several practice shots, and the bow was true and had a strong pull to it.

"Not bad!" said the soldier. Mark gave him back his sword; now, a new edge was placed on it.

Caleb was not prepared to hunt and kill Yeshuaians to save Eliza and Yael. Yet he remembered his parents telling him that the act of being a Yeshuaian often meant persecution for your beliefs. He also remembered learning that Paul had hunted and killed Yeshuaians before giving himself to the Messiah. Caleb's parents had promised him that the act of following Yeshua meant that he would be judged and found guilty of heinous acts. His choice many years ago to follow the teachings of Yeshua was now taking him to a place that he could never have imagined. He must now either kill or allow his cousin and a girl with the same name as his mother to be raped. It was a choice that no one should have to make.

"This is literally a choice between two bad endings! I will be like Paul or like Stephen," said Caleb.

The other soldier laughed, not knowing who either Paul or Stephen are. "You've killed before, kid. Listen, I have never met anyone who killed a centurion, as it takes a lot of battle prowess to earn the title of the centurion. You have what it takes. Let's just get this done. My family is getting a lot of money for this battle, and we really need the coin to make it through the rest of this winter before we can return to our farms north of here."

"So, you are from Gaul?" Caleb remembered his geography.

"I am. My grandfather was a druid, as was his father before him. We were all captured and enslaved during a Roman invasion several decades before I was born. My parents paid for our freedom, and they raised me with my two brothers north of here. Our family calls that place home now."

"Perhaps I can come to visit you once these battles are done, and you are free to return home," said Caleb, looking to calm his nerves. Hope for the future made sense in a pre-combat conversation. Hope for the future made sense in your relationship with Yahweh. That was also the message of the Messiah. Caleb was desperate for hope.

The Gaul extended his hand to Caleb. "My name is Ronan, from Gallia Cisalpina. The Roman idiots just call it Gaul."

At that moment, the portcullis was lifted, and two men twice Caleb's age came into view from identical gates on the other side of the pits. One man was armed with a bow, and the other held a sword and a spear. Neither wore any armor, helmets, or protective boots. Both had darker skin than any Roman or Gaul, and Caleb quickly concluded that they were from the lands of Palestine or like them. They were also seasoned combatants, and they would be faster than them, as they were unencumbered. Caleb realized that he was the only one fighting without previous experience. He needed an advantage.

But what would that be?

Circling above them all was an ominous murder of crows.

Caleb closed his eyes and felt another peace come over
him. He remembered Rabbi John's prophecy that birds would
fly above him as if they were a blessing. He smiled. Seeing the
prophecy gave him comfort. And he prayed a segment of one
of the first prayers he ever learned from his mother.

"Give us this day our daily bread and forgive us our
trespasses and we forgive the trespasser," he said in prayer.

He quickly recalled Ronan's plan. Ronan would step
out from the portcullis and begin trotting towards the two
men who they were supposed to kill. Caleb was to wait a
moment, then run at full speed to the right, circling behind
all the marble blocks that were part of the pit floor. He would
attempt to flank them while they were distracted by Ronan's
close-range threat of attack.

Ronan left without any prompting to do his part, and
the combatant wielding a bow launched his first arrow.
Ronan failed to stop it with his shield, and it struck him
between two rings in his chain mail, burying itself into his
chest with a loud thwack. Ronan grunted and fell, appearing
to have been killed instantaneously. Caleb watched Ronan
trying to move, but he lost his focus on his partner once an
arrow landed in the sand in front of him.

He responded with a defensive move. He climbed atop
a marble block that would afford some protection from
another arrow shot as the crowds erupted in glee at the flow
of fresh blood in front of Ronan. Caleb thought that once
this battle was complete, he needed to go to this man's home
and tell his family of his bravery.

Caleb knew that his opponent would be feeling a sense
of victory after receiving the crowd's applause. He notched
an arrow, jumped down from the marble block to the sand,
and ran at full speed in the direction that he thought they
would be going to flank him.

He had guessed right. They were not expecting one man to charge two men from the opposing flank. As they rounded a large block on the right side of the pits, Caleb was waiting for them. He put an arrow in the archer's upper thigh. The man went down immediately, and Caleb could see that the arrow had gone through bone and exited the other side of the leg. He would not be placing any load on that leg and would have to try to shoot without its support. Melee range weapons were now an advantage only to Caleb. If he can stay away and preserve his arrows, he can win. "Thank you, Yeshua," came from his lips, and he steadied himself to take another shot.

Caleb began counting his arrows as Rufus taught him to do. This act would keep him focused and mindful of his resources. That one arrow was not retrievable without first killing that man, leaving him with only five arrows remaining. Lightning fast, he notched another arrow and sent it into the armpit of the injured man, hearing him yell as the arrow ripped into his lung. He was not dead, but he would no longer discharge his bow this day. The battle for that man was also over, and the match was now even. Each team was down one man. His partner turned around and ran in the opposite direction from whence he came.

Caleb thought for a moment. He anticipated that the other combatant would lose his sense of advantage and be temporarily in shock. Caleb decided to waste an arrow and shot it in his direction to make it seem like he was pursuing him. Caleb hoped it would speed him up in the same way that tapping on a frog from behind makes him jump earlier. It worked, and Caleb ran directly at the spearman from a flanked position that the spearman was not looking. Once the man rounded a corner that should have provided him protection from Caleb, he was startled to see Caleb on one knee, directly in front of him at point-blank range. As the crowd erupted with joy, Caleb launched his arrow immediately upon seeing the white in the man's eyes. It struck his gut with full force, and it hung on the other side of his ribcage. He would not run again this day, and without any ranged weapons, Caleb had him.

Caleb decided to speak to the combatant, trying desperately to be heard over the deafening noises of the crowd.

"If I do not kill you, I risk losing my sisters!" Caleb involuntarily shouted at the gutted man, launching a second arrow into the man's gut on the opposite side. It made a loud thud when it hit, causing the crowd to erupt, and Caleb looked up only and saw that the emperor himself was standing up and cheering.

Caleb knew that the combination of those two wounds would be fatal soon, and he walked up to the wounded man and kicked the sword away from the man nearest to him. He pulled him across the sand and put him next to the first one. The crowds erupted, calling for a retributive strike by the injured man or for Caleb to decapitate him.

When they were next to each other lying on the sand, Caleb blocked out all the crowd noise and recommendations to commit atrocities. Instead, he spoke to them calmly in Hebrew.

"I am a member of The Way. The emperor requires that I kill you to save my family and protect my sisters' integrity. You must know that I do not wish to do this thing." He stood a spear's length away from where they both lay, in case either of them found the strength for a last lunging attack.

The one with the undamaged lungs responded. "We were boys about your age when the Solomon's Temple fell, and we were enslaved to serve in the Roman militia. If you take our lives, it will be an act of mercy. May our Messiah bless you and thank you for your gift of a speedy path to eternity with Him."

Caleb was shocked. These men were not just Jews but also believers in the Messiah. How could he kill them? He stood there, pondering his next move. He was paralyzed, just like his mother before him.

The crowd revolted at his inaction, and they began to chant, "Kill the Jews! Kill the Jews!" Caleb stood motionless in the pits of the Colosseum. A part of him wanted to scream out, but he knew to say nothing. Thought of his mother came back to him. Her honor was as much in his decision-making criteria as were their lives. He was not their judge. It was not his choice as to whether they must die or not.

Then, the emperor raised his hand, indicating that everyone be silent. He stretched his hand forward, with his palm facing down. This meant for the battle to end, there must be death. The emperor made his choice for him.

Caleb turned and screamed in the direction of Titus and his box, unaware that this act was forbidden. "Is this what you want? Is this what you and my uncle used to do? Is this what I must do to protect my sisters?" The crowd looked now not towards the pits and the battle there but at the emperor, awaiting his response. Caleb's public questioning of the emperor was worthy of death by crucifixion. Perhaps if Caleb knew that, he would not have done it. Titus gave him the benefit of ignorance.

The emperor's box was acoustically engineered so that anything he spoke would be heard down in the pits.

"Your uncle is dead, as you say," Titus replied. "You must make your choice. Will you choose to give me their lives, or shall I bed these sisters of yours?"

With that, the two soldiers in the emperor's presence pulled down the cloaks that were covering both Eliza and

Yael's upper bodies. Both girls attempted to cover their exposed breasts with their hands. "Leave yourselves uncovered until he has either killed the wretched Jews or has agreed that your flesh shall be mine," Titus said to them. The girls dropped their hands to their sides, causing laughter in the crowd and sheer rage inside Caleb.

He turned back towards Caleb, again extending the thumbs-down signal. The only decision to make now was to kill two Jews or allow himself to be killed. The emperor had just dispatched a squad of his most elite soldiers to the entrance to the pits to ensure that one of the two events occurred in a timely manner.

Caleb walked to the injured archer and took out his knife. He slit his throat the same way he killed the centurion a few weeks earlier. Caleb turned away as he heard blood pour out onto the sand, striking with enough force to make a noise. Killing a brother in Yeshua was not the same thing as killing a deer. Caleb was sick to his stomach. He held the man's head up with his hair until it went limp. Then he let go, and the man slumped over and hit the ground. He was dead.

The crowd burst into applause, and many of the royalty began to laugh. Caleb saw and heard nothing but the emperor. He looked up at him and yelled again with the full force of his lungs. "Is this what you want?" This time, there was no way that the emperor could have heard him.

Before Titus could respond, the remaining Jew spoke loud enough for Caleb to hear. The man was addressing God. "For Thine is the kingdom, the power, and the glory, forever and ever. Yeshua, take my soul that I may not trouble this world until You return in glory. Amen."

With tears in his eyes, Caleb slit the second man's throat, looking away to not see his last facial expression. His uncle warned him that the eyes of a dying man would invade the killer's dreams for years. Caleb looked up as the man went limp and saw that the emperor had allowed Eliza and Yael to get dressed.

Caleb felt more in that moment than at any time in his life. It was not at all like seeing his parents killed and returning the act with a retributive strike. It was much worse, as Caleb was now alone, covered in the blood of others who worshipped the same Yahweh as he did, and he must accept accolades for his efforts. It was unreconcilable. It was sickening.

Caleb's heart ached. This was not the kingdom of God that he had been promised. There was no glory from defeating the enemy in battle. Caleb knew that he would always remember the man's last words, even though he would never know the man's name.

When Caleb finally stood up, covered in the blood of his combatants, he saw the entire Colosseum giving him a standing ovation. The emperor was no longer in his box, meaning that he was probably heading down to the pit to meet Caleb himself.

Caleb saw that the two young boys had already run out and onto the pits. One of them handed him a towel while the other one pulled Ronan back into the cavern.

"He's not dead," said the boy.

"Mark, get him some help! I am going to speak with the emperor. And get this man's full name, his parent's name, and his hometown. I will come to find you later."

Caleb anticipated meeting the emperor and his entourage in a few moments.

Caleb ran back into the staging area to retrieve his stuff and get rid of the blood-soaked towel. He washed his face and hands and put his own sandals back on. He gave the boys a gold coin to relay to him the location and names of Ronan's hometown, and the boys gave him his untarnished cloak to put on.

"That was excellent work! Put this on, as you are about to meet the emperor," said Mark.

"I already have met that ugly camel. That is why I am here," he responded. He knew he shouldn't have said that, but he did not care what came with his offense.

In his quiver was exactly one arrow. It was the one he had practiced with, and he knew how it flew better than any of the others. He took it out and placed it on the bowstring, and began walking towards the emperor.

A NIGHT IN THE PALACE

The Colosseum had begun to empty, as theirs was the last event of the day. However, some stayed after to watch the equivalent of the awards ceremony. The winning gladiators always received great praise and rewards of coin and jewels for defeating a strong opponent. Those two had battled together nearly a hundred times, Caleb heard. The emperor had either set him up for failure or wanted a good fight. Caleb chose to believe that he knew that Rufus would only train the best kinds of soldiers.

As he walked towards the opposing portcullis, directly in front of him stood emperor Titus. Titus wore a crown of silver interlocking leaves and flowers. His cloak was not the one that he had worn in the bathroom some hours earlier but was adorned with golden threads and elaborate patterns, including royal purple hues.

Caleb had a choice to make. He wanted to launch his last arrow at Titus. Emperors rise to power and fall from it all the time. Why should his uncle's best friend be any different?

But he could not do it. He was the son of two murdered parents, and this was not the choice they would have wanted him to make. He had to kill those two Jews. He does not have to kill the emperor. Instead, he cast the bow to the ground, grumbling. Vengeance had not helped him the last time anyway.

"Good choice not to seek vengeance against the emperor," said Titus, clapping for Caleb as he approached.

Once Eliza heard the emperor speak at Caleb, she considered the environment safe again, and she ran from the back of the entourage and threw herself into Caleb's arms. He lifted her up and held her in the air, spinning her around two times, just like she had watched his aunt and uncle do. In Jewish culture, this was normally reserved only for married couples, but Eliza had lost any sense of her culture in this moment. She was grateful to have her family back.

"I prayed every moment you were gone," she whispered into his ear. Then, she kissed him on the cheek. "You protected me when you did not have to. You are a good man. I cannot imagine how difficult it was for you to do that."

Caleb picked her up and spun her again. "I had to do it for you. I did not have a choice that my mother would be proud of. You will be a good woman, one day! Today, I tried to make sure of that," he responded. She fully embraced him and spoke into his ears. "Cousin, thank you for loving me!"

The remaining crowd applauded them. "I think they think we are lovers or something," Eliza said.

"I do not know. Maybe they do." They both turned around to discover that the emperor was standing next to them.

"Your uncle trained you as I thought he might. Tonight, you are my guests at the palace," Titus said.

"So, will your keep your promise?" Caleb asked in a most confronting tone.

"I never made any promise to you."

Eliza knew that Titus was doing this to impress his entourage, and she suspected he was vulnerable to their sway. She spoke up again.

"Is it not true that the spoils of battle go to the winner?"

"So, the Hebrew girl speaks, again. Young man, you must discipline her for this."

"She speaks for me," said Caleb, honoring his cousin before the emperor. The emperor nodded, but neither of the children wanted to know his thoughts.

"Your Highness. I ask you to release the other Hebrew girl into my care," Eliza said with a risky tone of confidence. She gestured for Yael to come to her.

"In exchange, you may keep all the coin that otherwise goes to the victor," she offered.

The entourage looked at Titus and quietly whispered amongst themselves. She could tell that they loved this girl's aggressive stance upon victory and everyone awaiting the response of the King of the World. Titus also seemed impressed rather than offended by her presumptuousness.

"Very well, little one," he said, returning to his term of endearment. "I give you the Jewish girl and release her from her service to me and to the empire."

The entourage applauded the emperor as Yael left the back of the entourage and walked towards Eliza and Caleb. Yael dared not express any gratitude in front of any of them. Instead, she stepped behind Eliza and bowed her head, taking the place that a slave would normally occupy. Once everyone in the emperor's company had turned to leave, Eliza turned and gave Yael hugs and kisses like the one she gave Caleb. Caleb stood motionless as the two of them embraced. Yael was still scared and in shock, unable to speak.

"Come on, let's go. I need to wash up again. I still have blood on me. This is an awful feeling," said Caleb.

They began walking out of the Colosseum, quickly catching up to the entourage also going to the palace. Caleb stopped at the line to use the public washroom. Once he left, Yael finally spoke, but only to Eliza.

"I am indebted to you and am yours. I do not understand what just happened here," said Yael to Eliza gratefully.

"Caleb won, and I used his winnings to pay for your freedom. Caleb is completely uninjured, and we are leaving this disgusting place for the last time in our lives. That is what just happened!" said Eliza. The countenance on her face was of one filled with a peace that the world cannot understand. But it was calm, and Yael began to relax.

"I do not know what to say! Thank you! I hate this place, too," Yael said and laughed with a sense of great relief.

"Yael, you are not a slave anymore! Yahweh provided for your safety, not Caleb or me," she said.

With that final affirmation that they were both free, the girls returned to being girls as they waited for Caleb to get through the long line in the washroom. He came back a lot quicker than they thought.

"Everyone let me cut the line once they realized I was the guy who just fought. It was my first royal moment," he said. However, he shook his head and looked at the floor of the Colosseum as he put his hands on his hips.

"Let's get out of this place. I do not ever want to return," he said.

"We need to follow this group to the palace and do what this man says, so we can get what we need to help your parents get out of whatever they are in!" Caleb said in the angriest tone. Both girls stopped their play and agreed. The impact of the killings was starting to show in Caleb's countenance.

They followed the last of the soldiers and reached the palace grounds long before dinner. Titus disappeared, and three slaves approached the girls. The slaves were all old enough to be their mothers. "We are here to serve you and prepare you before tonight's events," said the first one.

"What events?" asked Eliza.

The slaves looked at each other. "We will help you get ready, yes?" she said. They left Caleb and walked into a small building filled with bathing rooms. It was adjacent to the main palace near the top of the Palatine Hill. Yael bit her tongue and decided not to explain to Eliza what she should expect at a royal orgy.

"Come with me, young master," said the remaining slave to Caleb, and she led him to a room adjacent to the girls. He found himself in a room with a large walk-in pool. The pool of water was larger than his family's kitchen back home.

"Please disrobe and enter the pool," said the slave. "You must be cleaned before tonight." Although he was protective of his cousin's public nudity, he had no such limitations on himself, and he quickly did as she said. "This is very nice," he said as he settled into the water. He closed his eyes and allowed all the tension from the day's combat to flow from his body and into the water. He was nearly nodding off when he felt his shoulders being rubbed.

He spun around and saw the slave woman rubbing his shoulders. "Please stop," he said, in Hebrew, not thinking if she would understand. Once he realized his mistake, he repeated himself in Greek, this time with a more gracious tone. She stepped back, as she was not in the pool but only on its edge.

"You are new to this place, yes?" asked another man, perhaps twice Caleb's age, who had just entered the pool himself. "I watched you in battle today, and it was obvious to all of us that you were not fighting for the sake of glory."

"Yes, this is very different than what I am used to," Caleb admitted.

"I do not have the courage to risk my life in the arena myself. The emperor told us that he gave you a choice, and you decided to fight. May I ask, what was the other choice?"

"You will need to ask the emperor if you want those details. They are a bit private; do not you agree?"

"Perhaps," said the man.

"Bring more hot water!" Immediately, two more slaves arrived carrying a large vat of steaming water. They poured it into the pool, and the temperature increased dramatically.

"Now that is more like it!" Caleb remarked, looking to change the subject. "I think I could get used to this."

"I have asked to be here with you, right now. I have a business deal for you." Caleb was not expecting this. Before he could react, the man began his pitch. "My house would like to sponsor you in the arena. We will pay you half a talent of gold for each victory. Couldn't your family use that coin?"

Remember my sisters out there? One of them carries about a talent of silver with her right now, and she can negotiate another half a talent when she sells a watermelon to an elephant. Why would I want to kill people for something we already have? Get out of here!

Those were the thoughts that came to his mind. But he did not voice them.

"I am not yet fourteen years old," he replied. "I wish to live my life to the fullest. I do not want to risk my future on a Colosseum battleground. I'm sure you understand."

"Very well," said the man as he climbed out of the water and left. "Live your life as you desire."

THE SIMPLICITY OF
THE MESSAGE

Eliza and Yael had received a similar bathing experience.
Their bath was also a walk-in, and the two older women came
into the tub with them. The older women scrubbed Eliza and
Yael's feet and hands, applying perfumes to their hair and
drying them off using Egyptian cotton towels that were the
size of blankets. The room they were in was more decorated
than some synagogues outside of ancient Jerusalem. Yael told
Eliza stories about how she used to serve in a bath like this
when she first arrived in the city before moving to Colosseum
services. She fell short of retelling her repeated raping in tubs
like this one, but Eliza could tell that the memories still hurt
her. She would need to talk to her about this more.

"Before I return home, I must buy some of these towels
to take both to my grandmother and my mother," Eliza said.
"They will love them."

As they finished drying off and removing the excess
frankincense, the two older women had them don pure white
robes laced with golden designs. Neither needed anything
done to their hair or nails, so they stepped into new sandals.

"I never thought I would wear one of these. Now, I
have!" said Yael.

"I had never even seen one until this morning. Now, I have worn two different ones on the same day!" said Eliza. "Yael, I have only known you a few hours, but I feel that I have known you my whole life," she added.

Caleb has chosen to embrace her as a reaction to the ultimatum placed on him by the emperor. Eliza felt that any sense of filter she had with Yael also needed to drop. If Caleb was a man of God and speaking the truth, this girl was now also her family, like it or not.

"I do not know what to say," said Yael, most bashfully. "I was a slave girl earlier today. Now, I am receiving your—" and with that, she broke down and began to cry. Eliza pulled her in, holding her like a young child who had just fallen down.

"I do not deserve the love that you and Caleb are showing me right now. I cannot understand this sentiment," she said.

"You know, Caleb started this. I know Caleb, and I know his mom and dad. He was angry when he called us sisters, but I know what he meant. You are now in our family. We are stuck with each other, now, like it or not!" said Eliza, trying to break the moment up. Since the older women did not understand Hebrew, they could only smile and listen to their gibberish.

"These robes do not cover all of us, and there are no undergarments to put on," Eliza noted uneasily. "Where are our ones from earlier? Even they cover more of me," she said.

"You can have it tomorrow," said the old woman.

"They are not intended to cover you as you are used to, as that impedes access to what is inside of them," Yael explained. Eliza paused when she figured out what Yael was alluding to. Her pause turned to shock. At that moment, the emperor walked in. He eyed the girls like a hungry wolf as he approached them.

Eliza knew what to do, just as she knew what to do when they were in the booth trying to see the emperor. Just like she knew what to do when Caleb went into combat. She prayed.

"Yeshua, only You are my Lord and King. This man has no authority not granted by You under heaven. Protect me from the evil one, and I know that the evil one is not here, right now. The emperor is not my enemy," she prayed. As she completed her prayer, she looked up and saw that the emperor was very close to her. Just like Caleb had chosen to overcome his paralysis, Eliza also did. She turned her head slightly and spoke to the man only a hand away from her face.

"You know, your childhood best friend, who is also my uncle, used to tell me stories of you. Would you like to hear one?"

"Sure," Titus replied indifferently. For her part, Yael remained next to Eliza, but she dared not move, fearing the wrath of a man she knew to be predatory.

"One evening, Rufus was recalling the days leading up to and immediately after the destruction of our Temple. He talked of the great siege engines that you made and the mass crucifixions. He spoke of entering the city and tearing down the great Temple that my ancestors treasured above all things except Yahweh Himself." Rufus was fascinated to see her ability to separate her feelings for her people's most holy place from his actions from fourteen years earlier.

It was hard for her to gauge whether Titus was really listening to her, but she knew that he needed to hear this message. "And you know what he said he felt afterward? He said he felt nothing. He had started in the Roman military, just as his father before him, and he was now the legate over a legion of soldiers who had done something that no Roman military had ever succeeded in accomplishing. He said that he was at the top of the world, wouldn't you agree?"

"Almost at the top. I remained above him!" Titus chuckled to himself. With that, Eliza returned briefly to her prayer, then she continued.

"You were. He said you were a great leader and great friend. He said that you gave him permission to take any spoils that he wanted. He had enough wealth to build a palace anywhere in the empire. Perhaps even two of them. But then, he made the greatest decision of his life. That is what he calls it. After meeting my uncle Mishi and learning the truth about the Messiah, he agreed to leave his post in the Roman military, retire from his service, and join my aunt and uncle in their pursuit of what truly matters. He stayed behind and protected my family as they ministered to people in the area surrounding ancient Jerusalem. Most Jews did not know yet that the Messiah had come. They thought there would be a spirit that would come to rid us of the Roman Empire, as there had been other great Hebrews in the past who had redeemed us. But the Messiah who was sent came not to rid us of Roman occupation. The Messiah who was sent came to rid us of death caused by our sins."

The emperor seemed to be losing interest.

"Uncle Rufus said that the two of you exchanged many letters after you separated," Eliza said, attempting to regain his full attention.

"We did, but I do not remember what he said. That was many years ago."

"I know my uncle's heart. I am sure he asked you if you were happy or not. Did he ever invite you to come back to

Jerusalem and meet the church that he served in?" She knew that he had, as she had read copies of Rufus' letters.

"Yes, he did." The emperor was now becoming introspective, and both of the girls could see it. A nerve had been touched.

Eliza felt emboldened. It was as if she was made for this moment. "Uncle Rufus knew that your love of flesh and of war could be replaced with a joy fuller than those things. He loved you enough to share that with you. I know he missed you. He told me that when he took care of me when I was a young girl."

The emperor stepped away from both of them, and his form went nearly limp. He did not know what to say. He began to see the evil of an act of taking her flesh as it was the property of his brother, and it dawned on him that this act was wrong. He moved away from his position near her to a safer distance, signifying respect.

"You are not like any of the other Hebrew girls who have served in this place," Titus said, lightly hyperventilating.

"Perhaps. But I am here to serve you right now with the most powerful truth in the history of the world. I can sense that you want to know what it is. Rufus needed it. I need it. Would you like to hear the greatest story ever told?"

"Yes, I do. Tell me!"

Eliza asked the emperor to sit down, and she told him the story of Yeshua. As she told the story, she continually remembered how her aunt would speak, mixing in powerful words from the Creator with light humor and personal stories. The words came naturally to her, and she was at great peace. Eliza prayed, thanking Jehovah for the chance to be present for this moment. Perhaps all of history would change. But for her, it was only her history that she could sincerely impact. At every moment she spoke, Eliza saw that she was not only replicating her auntie's words, but she also replicated her tone and her body language. Her aunt had a few phrases that she repeated and built her life upon. This moment was an application of those words. And in this moment, Eliza migrated from student to teacher as she shared with the emperor.

"Confronting those who wish to harm you with truth and love is the only sincere way to approach life," is what her aunt would say.

In her soul, she again felt the resonance that her aunt told her about. It was the same resonance from last week. It made both the emperor and the two girls smile.

And it felt good.

THE MORNING AFTER

Eliza awoke with Yael, as the two of them had slept in the same bed. Caleb was asleep on the floor next to them. As they began to stir, the servants entered, offering them chamber pots to relieve themselves.

An older woman came in carrying a concoction of herbs and oils, offering it to the girls.

Eliza took one smell and gave a face of total disgust. Yael raised her hand, saying, "No, thank you," to the older woman.

"This is to prevent pregnancy," she said. "The emperor spent much of the night with you two. I am sure you need it," she said.

Yael repeated, "No, thank you," but Eliza was the one to speak up.

"He never touched us. We were not violated," she said.

"Yes, of course," said the old lady as she turned and walked away.

"The emperor will not support these children you will have with him," she said as she walked out.

Eliza and Yael giggled, and Caleb spoke for the first time this morning.

"We need to get out of this place," Caleb said. "I almost died yesterday, and you two spent the night talking with the

Emperor of the World. What is going on in our lives?" he asked.

Yael called for a servant since she knew the operating protocol for communication in the palace. She asked him to send a message to the docks to request a boat to take them back to Judah by the fastest means possible. A young runner left the palace to secure three seats on the afternoon vessel. Another runner brought Caleb a note containing all the information regarding Ronan that he had asked for.

They washed and walked to the top floor of the central building, as they had been instructed. On the rooftop sat the emperor and his Hebrew concubine. He was completing his morning calisthenics. "Keeps a man young," he said as they came into view. "You know, last night was the first night since I became emperor that I did not bed a woman." Both girls looked at the concubine, looking for some sign from her, but they got nothing.

"I have never bedded a woman," said Caleb with a hint of disdain. He still did not like Titus, even after hearing that he had heard and asked many questions about the Messiah the night before. Titus had made him kill, and he remained enraged by the emperor's display of power over him.

"Titus, would you please give me what I need to get my parents back?" Eliza asked. She addressed him using his name and not his office, an act of great intimacy. The emperor smiled at them and laughed.

"Young Hebrews, you had it the whole time," Titus replied, throwing Caleb back his uncle's ring. "If you carry the confidence that you had down in those pits and wear the ring showing your family's authority, my soldiers will comply with your requests. They will help you find them. You did not need to come to me."

Titus paused, clearly contemplating something. Then, he spoke to Caleb in an eager voice. "Once you find them, you need to come back here to train with my elite cadets. I can already tell that you are not going to fight in the pits again, but I think you could be a great trainer for future generations of soldiers. If you are interested in this."

Caleb knew this to be another assertation of power and control. This time, though, Caleb was in control. Caleb smiled but did not speak.

While he spoke to Caleb, he handed Eliza a sealed scroll. He then turned and addressed her as she looked at it.

"This has the emperor's seal on it. It instructs anyone in possession of your parents to release them. Do not lose it."

"Thank you," she said.

The five of them sat down to a cheerful breakfast, each pleased with how the events of the day were unfolding. Soon, the runner came back before their meals were complete, saying that their boat was ready now if they wished to leave.

Eliza took out two silver coins from her inner purse and handed them to the runner. "There is a man in the marketplace named Balbi. He sailed over with us. Tell him that we have departed and hope to see him again. Tell him he is also free."

"I told him two nights ago. That was between Yahweh, him, and me," Caleb finished, not wanting to say more. Eliza remembered the look on his face when John was talking, and she understood.

"Your Highness, it is time for us to depart," Caleb said respectfully. "Thank you for your help," The two men exchanged a warriors' departures, just as Uncle Rufus had taught Caleb to do. He hated the man, yet he wanted to hug him at the same time.

Yael and Eliza bowed, and the three went to leave, but Titus stopped them, looking into Eliza's eyes thoughtfully. "What do I call you, young teacher?" he asked.

"I am only Eliza. I am pleased that you are open to His offer of eternal life. Perhaps we can talk again. My sister Yael has already sent a message to her local synagogue, and the rabbi there will come and speak with you each week, as you desire. There are also many men in the prison who have a great understanding of the Messiah and His message. The man who taught my auntie spent many years in your prisons, and many of his followers are still there, Titus." Her authority in the moment was undeniable, and it was obvious that Titus would do what she said.

"Can you be my rabbi?" Titus asked, almost as if he were a child making a request to his mother.

Eliza smiled but shook her head. "For now, I must find my parents. I am still young, and there are others living very near to you who understand the message of eternal life given us by Yeshua. You must get to know them. I must leave you now."

Titus nodded and signaled to a servant standing at the top of the stairs. The servant brought over an ornately carved box made of the finest acacia wood and opened it. Inside was a golden ring that bore the insignia of the house of Flavian of which Titus was a member. "Take it. Wear it the next time you come here, and you will not have any problems. You are now a member of my house. My brother Domitian has already been told, as well. I claim you as family."

"Thank you," she said, picking the ring up and putting it on the middle finger of her left hand. Yael shook her head in disbelief. They bowed again and left.

Yael could not contain herself. "I now know two women who are rabbis!"

"Shut up," said Eliza among their laughing. The little children inside of the two girls could come out again. The reason for their journey had reached fruition, and it was time for the long boat ride back to Judea. It was time to go home.

Yael stopped them both.

"Would you two look down at your hands?" she asked, as each of them did.

"You each wear a ring of significance. You, Caleb, did not know that you already had what you needed. You, Eliza, have what you do not need. I have the gift of freedom, and I would not trade it, now that I know what it is like not to have it, for either of your rings!"

"Woah, that is a bit too deep for me!" said Caleb in jest.

"I do not know...I just might need mine when we get back home. It will make telling stories back home a bit more believable," Eliza said.

"Eliza, you are so stupid, you know that?" said Caleb.

"Let's go to the market and get some of that Egyptian cotton. Then, we are getting on a boat and sailing home," she said.

"Can I have some of your coins?" asked Yael. "I want to get some things for my family, especially my little sister. She had probably grown up a lot since I have been gone," she said.

"Sure, you can have all you want," she said.

"You are unbelievable!" said Caleb. "When I ask for your coin to get something, you give me an evil eye. Yael shows up, and you give her whatever she wants. This is just not fair."

"She is my sister. You told the emperor yourself, yes?" she said, sounding and acting just like his mother.

Caleb turned around in disgust and began walking towards the markets. The two girls locked their arms together, grabbed their bags, and followed behind him. They were laughing when Caleb abruptly stopped. He turned around and ran back.

"I forgot my stuff," he said, laughing. "Wait for me!" he said.

The girls began laughing again.

"If he is going to be your family, you will need to get used to him doing stuff like this," Eliza said.

She completely missed the look on Yael's face when she called him family.

THE TRIP HOME, ALL WITH NEW FAMILY

They were emotionally wired when they got on the boat, and Eliza showed her ring to the captain of the new boat. He did not care. He was not like their first captain, as she had hoped he would be. The two deckhands were equally distant, and the best she could gather is that all of them were supposed to have a week off when they found out that they were given a surprise sailing to operate. They did not want to be there.

The two girls were pleased to find that they had their own cabin. Caleb shared a cabin with a Hebrew man from Joppa. There was another older Jewish couple, but they were ill and seeking passage home to die and be buried with their ancestors. They seldom spoke to anyone and spent most of their days below deck.

Their trip down the west coast of the empire was uneventful, but as soon as they turned east to go through the Strait of Messene, a storm reached that part of the Mediterranean, forcing their vessel to spend three nights at the port of Messene on the Island of Sicily. Caleb wanted to get a dinghy to take him across the strait so that he could thank the rabbi in Reggio, but neither the captain nor the swells in the strait would allow for it. Instead, the three of them spent nearly all of their time talking to the locals and staying warm by the fire at the inn.

They got to know each other well, with Yael learning about Caleb's parents' entire background as well as his family history. Yael's family was from a Hebrew farming village not far from the coast, and they had to sell her into slavery after marauders attacked and destroyed their harvest and took what they needed to pay taxes. It was obvious that Caleb was enraged at the thought of selling Yael into slavery for lack of any other choice, but there was no sense of vengeance in his responses. Eliza hoped that her cousin was healing, but he did not have any sense of peace about him. She prayed for him, often.

For her part, Eliza remained elusive in her tales of her village, fearing that Caleb and Yael would begin asking questions about her obvious wealth, and she was not ready to tell them the whole story. Indeed, she did not have permission to, either. With inclement weather keeping them indoors, they learned some Roman games to pass the time, and they all consumed lots of tea and drank more soup.

After four days in the port of Messina, they departed and continued to Joppa. They left a letter to the rabbi with the harbormaster to deliver the next time a boat crossed the strait.

On the last section of the ride, Caleb and Eliza continued their storytelling with Yael. Despite the hurt that Caleb and Eliza experienced by seeing their family members killed and captured, Yael had to endure greater calamities as a slave at the house of one of the royal families. As she told stories, Eliza would often hold her and let her weep bitter tears that had been bottled up with each trauma building on top of the next. Caleb and Eliza both shared their times in the house of healing with Yael, and they both told her that she needed to go there with them when she returned. Caleb recounted what he learned from Rabbi Dor, and Eliza pointed out there were mysteries that she did not understand that the healing rabbis would help her with. They both promised to take her there. It took several iterations over several days to convince Yael to go there with them; her only request was that she should go home and see her mother and little sister first.

The days were beginning to lengthen again, and Yael was not able to sleep. She went on the deck to see the stars and let the waves rock her to drowsiness. At the front of the boat stood Caleb, wrapped in his royal cloak that he got for the Colosseum. He looked like the men in Rome, but she knew that he wasn't. She saw a man willing to put himself in harm's way for her. Most other men expected her to be harmed for them. She knew this man was from God. This man was part of her prayers that were being answered.

"You cannot sleep, either?" he asked as she approached.

"No," she said.

Without hesitating, Caleb put his arm around her and pulled her into his chest, in the same way that he would do with Eliza. He kissed her on the top of her head, just like he did with Eliza.

"You know, when I told the emperor that you were my sister, I did that for my mom," he said. Yael pushed him away the slightest amount, so she could look up and see into his eyes.

"You know, my mom got raped by a Roman soldier. They just told me that story less than a month ago. I was so mad. When I saw that my parents and my uncle were killed, I killed in response. That was such a stupid choice. The act of killing has haunted me more than seeing my father take his last breath. That is why I cannot sleep," he said.

"Oh, Caleb, I am so sorry," she said, leaning back into his chest. She wrapped her arms around his chest and molded into him. He rocked her until both of them were ready for sleep. After a few more moments, Caleb motioned towards the stairs, and the two of them headed down to their quarters.

Yael lay in her bed, unable to sleep still, as Caleb was now on her mind.

BACK IN JUDAH

When they arrived back in Judah, the port of Joppa seemed no different than before they had left.

"This place hasn't changed one bit," said Yael as they got off the boat. "Everything here looks the same as if nothing has happened." What she meant was that her home had not changed as much as she had changed. This timeless fact of growing up was only now apparent to the teenaged girl. She had already seen a lifetime of miraculous events, but she did not really understand the impact yet.

Eliza looked out and saw a reason for new hope. A quarter of everyone in view were slaves, and there was no evidence of any reason to live other than to make money. Commerce was everywhere, but all she thought of was how the world would be different with a new emperor, filled with the Holy Spirit.

"I can only imagine how the world will change now that the emperor has accepted Yeshua as his Messiah," said Eliza.

"I hope he closes the Colosseum for gladiator battles. That experience really messed me up. I still want to destroy that place," Caleb said. He was obviously upset at hearing the name of the emperor. He paused then changed the topic, hoping to change his heart.

"You know, that was a crazy thing you did," said Caleb, shaking his head in newfound disbelief. "I do not even think my mother would have done that, you know, witnessing to the emperor when he was about to take your virginity."

"My aunt most certainly would have!" said Eliza, defending her aunt's courage. They all laughed as they stepped off the boat and back onto dry land.

"Oh, this dock feels so good!" said each of them, in their own ways. Eliza tipped the deckhands, and the three of them clapped, celebrating a wreck-free boat tide.

With their bags unloaded and placed onto the docks, Caleb walked down the docks to look for porters to carry their gear to the wagons on which they would begin their inland journey. The girls walked a few steps behind him and chatted with each other happily. Joppa felt calm after the bustle of Rome. Best of all, they could understand everything that was being said around them, and they were standing on land. They stopped at the end of the docks and waited for Caleb to come back from the crowds.

Caleb returned with a look of horror on his face. "Guess what I just heard from the soldiers? The emperor is dead! The soldiers patrolling the docks now said that a note came in, announcing that he died of a sudden disease. I cannot believe it!"

Yael and Eliza stood with Caleb, equally stunned. Caleb called over the soldier who he had been speaking to so that they could get more information. "When did this happen?" he asked the man. "We were literally just there in his palace two weeks ago. And how did that message get to Judah so quickly?"

"You were in his palace? You are Jews! How is that possible?" the soldier asked.

"Long story. Eliza, hold up your hand," commanded Caleb. Eliza released part of her grasp on Yael and lifted her left hand, exposing the ring on her middle finger, signifying her membership in the Flavian house and a member of Titus' family.

The soldier shook his head while he grunted a few expletives before continuing.

"A couple of ships left from Rome the day he died with sealed decrees on each boat from the new emperor declaring Titus' death and Domitian's claim to the throne. They stopped along the way to hand copies of the decrees to dockmasters in all the major ports of the Mediterranean. None of the crew ever disembarked. They just kept sailing. They sailed in here the day before yesterday. They even sailed through a storm in the Strait."

After the guards initiated some small talk about the palace and what it was like to enter it, Caleb refocused the conversation. Caleb knew what to do with shock. He needed to focus.

"We are looking for her parents," Caleb told the soldier while motioned toward Eliza. "They were captured, and we have permission from the old emperor to free them."

"Good luck with that, considering the guy who gave that order is now dead."

"Who did you say was the new emperor?" asked Eliza rhetorically.

"The note said Domitian, Titus's younger brother," said the soldier.

"Great. Same house, same family. Same ring. We did not meet him, but Titus told me that he sent him a message that I am a member of his house," said Eliza, making eye contact both with Caleb and Yael while wearing her best smile. She, too, had learned the power of action when feeling paralyzed.

The soldier shook his head in disbelief and picked a new tone.

"Have you also gone to the top of Mount Olympus and had tea with Zeus, as well?" he asked with great sarcasm.

The girls laughed, and Caleb reached forward to grab the man's shoulder. Despite the law mandating that no Hebrew may touch a Roman soldier on duty, Caleb knew this guy would dare not unsheathe his blade to strike a member of the house of the emperor.

"Tell us where to go to get information about her mother's whereabouts," Caleb asked in a soft-spoken tone. The soldier was aware that these three adolescents were his superiors and responded in kind.

"I would say that you should go to the dockmaster and ask to meet with the commerce director. He is responsible for all slave traffic in Judah. He can tell you who to talk to in that region."

"Thanks. We need a couple of porters to get our stuff, and we need to rent a cart to travel inland for a couple of days. Any recommendations?"

The soldier pointed them to a small shack near the first docks where men were lined up, looking to make some money by carrying luggage and baggage. Caleb went to the end of their dock with the girls, telling them to wait there while he got a couple of boys not much younger than he was to gather their gear. He gave two copper coins each to pick up their bags and load them on a wagon and driver he had just rented. The dockhands came back with only four of their six bags, and Eliza quickly realized that it was her bags that were missing. She ran around the dock area, interrogating everyone she saw, but it was no use. They were gone.

After several minutes of this, she gave up and put her head on Caleb's chest, letting bitter tears fall.

"Those bags contained the box the emperor gave me and about 40 percent of the gold coin we got from the cinnamon sales. My mom and grandmother's cotton towels were in there, and some new pots for my family's kitchen. What are we going to do?" Eliza had been anticipating a joyous return home and had filled the bags with gifts for her family and the school that remained in Tamar. She wanted to show the village mayor all the profit she made in Rome. Now, she had nothing to give to the people she loved that looked up to other than stories.

She did not tell the entire truth. She now feared that she did not have enough coins to get them all around Judah as they looked for her parents. She felt responsible for the threat of financial shortcomings. Money was important to her, and it was taken from her, and much of the fault was her own.

Yael leaned her head on Eliza's back, but Caleb saw that she needed affirmation too. He pulled both of them into him. When one cried, so did the other. When the tears stopped, Eliza dropped any sense of filter on her mouth and spoke.

"Yael, you are the best thing that happened to me on this trip. I am sure we will find my parents, and Yahweh will answer my prayer. But I could not have done this without you to talk to. Truly, both of us were in grave danger these last days. You are a most unexpected friend, Yael," she said.

"Only a few members of the synagogue knew of my conditions. Most people only saw the clothing on the outside and the location of my services; they did not know what those men did to me. We prayed every time we gathered that Yeshua would send me a hope that I could return to normal life one day. You know what? He sent me *you*."

The two girls hugged again. Caleb knew that this would end soon, so he tolerated their public display. However, when Yael saw Caleb staring at her, she smiled and stared back, with no intention of breaking her gaze with him.

"You two done?" Caleb asked.

It was obvious to Yael that Caleb did not want to get caught by Eliza casting his eyes into hers. There could be no public display of chemistry. He was not ready for that. He knew how competitive Eliza could be, and Eliza needed Yael more than he did. Yael needed healing, as her understanding of sex and men was warped and needed fixing.

Caleb felt like he needed to say something in this moment. Something important. He did not need to be thinking about a future with Yael.

"We have survived the trauma of death and kidnapping. We have survived a shipwreck and an attempted rape. We have seen horrors. I have killed multiple men, including my brethren in Yeshua."

He looked around and continued, as his father would often do.

"All the while, God has blessed us with great good. We received blessings from a foreign rabbi we were not expecting to meet. We have seen how enthusiastic the underground synagogues in Rome are, and they are growing under the watch and support of the Roman military, of all things. We spent the night in the palace of the emperor and left with his favor. And we have witnessed the greatest conversion to Yeshua since Saul himself became Paul. We are truly blessed by Jehovah Jireh. Why are we upset about some Egyptian towels and coin?" The girls laughed and nodded in agreement.

"Come on, let's go see the dockmaster," said Caleb, and he turned and was about to start walking away when Yael jumped into the lead role in the conversation.

"This is the craziest week any Hebrew woman has experienced since Mary herself gave birth to the Messiah! I know you guys have a different plan, but can we go back to the inn, have a meal, and sit by the fire for a little bit. We need to celebrate a safe return."

All three of them laughed. They needed to laugh.

"Agreed, but first, let's check with the dockmaster," said Caleb.

They first stopped at the dockmaster's shack and asked to go over his logs of import and export records, along with all associated tariffs. He saw the ring on Eliza's hand and offered them no resistance, nor did he charge them for his time. For the rest of the afternoon, they reviewed all records since they had left a month and a half ago. No slaves had left this port with the names Katya and Matthew. That meant Eliza's parents were still in Judah.

They turned from the wharf area and headed to the inn to celebrate the success of the first half of their trip.

THE NEXT CHOICE, BUT NOT THE LAST CHOICE

After the meal and some chatter, all of them looked out a window and saw that the sun would be setting soon. Caleb shared a room with a merchant, and Eliza and Yael got one of their own. The three of them sat by the fire in the main hall and talked until dinner was ready.

They began a debate about what to do next. After a few iterations, they all agreed that finding Eliza's parents was the reason they went to Rome, but they had to do two things first. They decided that their next step was to stop at Yael's village then go on to the house of healing. Eliza and Caleb knew that they were not emotionally prepared to return to Tamar to discover what they might not be ready to handle. The attack had happened a month and a half ago, and the Romans involved were certainly not going to stick around afterward, but the families that Caleb and Eliza knew would be there, and they would have to mourn with them again. They knew that Matthew and Katya could be anywhere, but if they could wait six weeks to be freed, they could wait for one more. Figuring out where to begin their search was the hardest part because they would need to return to Tamar first to pick up the trail. Yael's hometown was on the way to the house of healing, so they all agreed to stop there first.

The emotional events that occurred that day exhausted all of them, and they retired to their rooms not long after sunset. They had been traveling east for many days, and it was impacting their perception of day and night. Even after telling Yael of the events that were haunting him, Caleb's sleep remained impacted by his dreams, and he seemed to be reliving the combat in the Colosseum literally every day.

"I have got to talk to the rabbis about killing the other Yeshuaians in the gladiator pits. I cannot sleep without reliving it," he said to both of the girls. Both he and Eliza feared that his emotional exhaustion would cause him to unsheathe his sword and kill someone in a moment of rage. No one wanted that.

For her part, Eliza did not think she needed help, and when Caleb suggested that she needed to sort out her sexual assault, she said that she had already done it with Yael. Caleb did not bring it up again, but he thought there was more to her story that needed to be told. He did ask Yael the same question, and Yael agreed with him, thinking Eliza needed help in the same way that she did. When a man forces himself on you sexually, you need help, regardless of his success.

For her part, Yael looked at two people who had been complete strangers two weeks ago. Now, they were part of her family. Soon, they would travel to her village and meet her family. She did not fear their judgment. She had first-hand experience of how they treated strangers. But she did not know what the circumstances in her home might be these days. She buried her feelings for Caleb for the moment and decided to invest in their joint relationship.

"We need people like you two. The world needs people like you two. You know, most of our story is unbelievable.

Caleb, you were offered the most lucrative deal a fighting man could ever dream of, and you walked away. Eliza, you were offered literally anything you wanted, and you said, 'No, thank you,' and you got on a boat with me for two weeks eating only soup, instead!" All of them laughed.

"I was freed from captivity by your spontaneous gift. Obviously, I have guilt in that I cannot repay you. Fortunately for me, you do not want repayment, and you do not make me feel guilty. However, now I must return to the people who sold me and try to love them. I am grateful you are traveling with me, as this return to my home village scares me. I am scared of my father when he sees me," she said.

Yael paused, biting her lip. She knew that the truth in the moment was not their stories. It was her stories of escape from captivity into the arms of people committed to treating her like family. They extended every gift they had, most especially their personal vulnerability. She had seen their strengths, but she also knew their weaknesses.

Yael, too, was a seeker. She sought connection. She sought family, and like most who have gone before her, she failed to see that the connections she needed to make were the ones in front of her. For the last year and a half, she yearned to be home more than anything on the earth; in reality, she was as home with Eliza and Caleb as she was in her hometown.

As they walked to their rooms, Caleb took ownership of the role his father had as head of household and head of the family. He also took ownership of his developing sexuality and his fondness for Yael. As the girls stood outside the room, Caleb reached over and interlocked his fingers with Yael's. Eliza looked down at Caleb's move, then looked at the two of them. Yael was obviously experiencing something, and she stood motionless. Caleb took her other hand.

275

Eliza turned to walk away, but Caleb said, "No, stay. You are my family now, and our laws state that family is supposed to be a part of this process."

Eliza walked and stood next to Caleb.

"Yael, we are not okay. You have been repeatedly raped, and I have killed too many men in the last month, most of whom did nothing other than follow orders. We need help. However, I think Yahweh placed us all together. My cousin needs you, but when I am with you, I see that I am not complete without the affirmation you give me. Perhaps one day we can complete each other if you are interested in such a thought," he said.

Caleb had no idea what he was doing. Hebrew culture mandates that the family be involved in the process of selecting a mate. Eliza was his only family, and she did not know what he was doing, either.

Eliza nodded her head but said nothing. Normal families look for girls who have followed the faith and are pure. Caleb's parents' own story convinced him that these ancient ways were no longer comprehensive. God can and has used everyone and everything for good. He had just now decided that Yael was no exception.

"Yes, I think I could explore that with you," she said.

Caleb turned to Eliza and asked for her opinion.

"I, um, I do not know. No, I do know. Yahweh has placed all of us together, just as you said. What we are all supposed to do remains unknown, except for what is next. I like the idea that you are exploring the idea."

"Eliza, we are not leaving you, or I am not leaving you," Caleb said.

Yael saw the intimacy of this moment was no longer between her and Caleb. It included Caleb's family. She knew that his world would need to start anew once Eliza found her parents. It would start anew even if she did not find her parents. Yael wanted to be a part of that.

"Eliza, I also am not leaving you," said Yael. He pulled both girls into his chest for a final embrace before bed.

Caleb's feelings no longer made sense. He called both of them sisters before the emperor, and it nearly cost him his life. Yet, neither of them was only a sister. Eliza was his adventure mate, and every great story in his life so far included her. She handled their wealth, and she spoke of the greatest story with confidence. She was there when he learned about his mother's rape and could not imagine ever talking to Yael about his feelings and not including her. Perhaps this is how a family is meant to be during the early stages of erusin. He had no one to help him through this other than her.

Eliza had known ever since Caleb looked at the dancing girls at the house of healing that he was interested in girls. She knew that without parents, he would find it difficult to pick a spouse. She was hoping that he would include her in the process, even if she did not really know how to pick a good bride from a bad one. She told herself she would support him when the day came. She did not think it would be today.

Yael did not know what she felt. Caleb literally risked his life for her, and he was beyond reproach with his duties as head of household, protector, and provider. He certainly looked nothing like the older, pale-skinned men who molested her this last year. But she could not imagine being with him and having his children, ever. The thought created terror. She needed hope that she could overcome these things.

"Good night," he said. He closed their door as an act of protection and left to go to his room.

"How long has this been going on?" Eliza asked.

"One moment," Yael said. Not true, but true enough. "And, I am scared," she said.

"Caleb doesn't know what he is doing, you know that, right?" said Eliza. Yael only nodded as they lay in their bed together.

"I do not either. My parents need to be involved in this. That is the way."

Eliza looked up to the ceiling and blew out their candles. In the dark, she spoke one last time.

"We will all have to figure this out together. If we can get an audience with the emperor and all of us leave as family, we can certainly figure out this…whatever it is."

"And I really like Caleb's choice in girls," Eliza ended.

"And I do not really know what is happening. This day has been crazier on my heart than any day in Rome. For sure, I need healing from my past, as do you and Caleb. Tomorrow is going to happen sooner than you think, and we still have work to do. Let's pray and go to sleep."

The Seeker's Trilogy concludes with adventures of healing and finding a home as Eliza, Caleb and Yael finish their journeys. The final book in the trilogy, Of Healing and Finding Home, is scheduled for release in the summer of 2021.

CPSIA information can be obtained
at www.ICGtesting.com
Printed in the USA
JSHW040813170621
15979JS00002B/3